RISING★STARS

MEDAL MATHS

Year 3

Practice Textbook

By
Jane Bovey

```
Medal Maths Practice Textbook Year 3
   This is not a photocopiable book.
```

Rising Stars UK Ltd., 76 Farnaby Road, Bromley, BR1 4BH
www.risingstars-uk.com

Every effort has been made to trace copyright holders and
obtain their permission for the use of copyright material.
The authors and publishers will gladly receive information
enabling them to rectify any error or omission in
subsequent editions.

All facts are correct at time of going to press.

Published 2004
Text, design and layout © Rising Stars UK Ltd.

Editorial: Tanya Solomons
Concept design: Marc Burville-Riley
Design: Clive Sutherland
Illustrations: © Clive Sutherland and Marc Burville-Riley
Cover design: Marc Burville-Riley

British Library Cataloguing in Publication Data
A CIP record for this book is available from the British
Library.

ISBN 1-904591-40-X

Printed by Cromwell Press, Wiltshire, UK.

Contents

How to use this book

Medal Maths has been created to provide pupils with a complete series of questions to support the whole National Numeracy Strategy Framework. There are three different levels of questions: Bronze, Silver and Gold.

Answers are available in the Medal Maths Teacher's Book Year 3.

Explanations
Explanations and examples are given for each objective to support children working independently.

Medal Standard	Objective Level
Bronze Medal Questions	**NNS Year 2**
Silver Medal Questions	**NNS Year 3**
Gold Medal Questions	**NNS Year 4**

Pupil's Notes

Practice and more practice is the best method for getting results and improving your performance in Maths.

For the best results:

a) Read the explanation.

b) Complete the questions at the most appropriate level.

c) Use the hints and tips to help you.

d) See if you can complete the next level of questions!

Bronze Medal Questions
These questions are set at the level expected for Year 2 as presented by the NNS Framework.

Silver Medal Questions
These questions are set at the expected level for Year 3 as presented by the NNS Framework.

How to use this book

National Numeracy Strategy
Every area of the NNS is covered (including all the Mental Maths objectives).

Objective
Each objective is covered through an explanation, three levels of questions and hints and tips.

---

6 Numbers and the number system

Describing number sequences

Ten athletes are lining up to start a race. They all have to be in order but some of them have forgotten to wear their numbers.

136, 137, ☐, 139, 140, ☐, 142, 143, ☐, 145, ☐

Runners 138, 141, 144 and 146 have forgotten to put on their numbers.

Look at the runners lining up for the following races.
See if you can work out which ones have forgotten to wear their numbers.

Bronze

1. 78, ☐, 80, ☐, 82, 83, ☐, ☐, 86, ☐

2. 61, ☐, 63, ☐, ☐, 66, 67, ☐, ☐, 70

3. 45, 44, 43, ☐, 41, ☐, 39, 38, ☐, ☐

4. 98, ☐, 96, ☐, ☐, 93, 92, ☐, 90, ☐

5. ☐, 54, 55, ☐, ☐, 58, 59, ☐, 61, ☐

Silver

1. 148, 149, ☐, 151, ☐, ☐, ☐, 154, ☐, 156

2. 197, 198, ☐, ☐, 201, ☐, ☐, 204, ☐

3. 176, 175, 174, ☐, ☐, 171, ☐, ☐, 168

4. 123, ☐, ☐, 126, ☐, 128, ☐, ☐, ☐, 132

5. ☐, 116, ☐, 114, 113, ☐, ☐, 110, ☐

Gold

1. 789, ☐, ☐, 792, ☐, ☐, 195, ☐, ☐

2. 654, ☐, ☐, 651, ☐, ☐, 648, ☐, ☐, 645

3. ☐, ☐, 943, 944, ☐, 946, ☐, ☐, 949, ☐

4. ☐, 499, ☐, ☐, 502, ☐, ☐, ☐, 506,

5. ☐, ☐, ☐, 879, 878, ☐, ☐, ☐, ☐, 872

 Training Tips

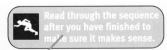 Read through the sequence after you have finished to make sure it makes sense.

 Check first to see if the sequence is going up or down.

Gold Medal Questions
These questions are set at the level expected for Year 4 as presented by the NNS Framework.

Questions
There are more than 2000 questions covering all the NNS Objectives.

Hints and Tips
Hints and tips support lower ability students and help to consolidate learning.

Sport Theme
The sport theme is often used within the questions to put the maths into context.

Describing number sequences

Ten athletes are lining up to start a race. They all have to be in order but some of them have forgotten to wear their numbers.

136, 137, ☐, 139, 140, ☐, 142, 143, ☐, 145, ☐

Runners 138, 141, 144 and 146 have forgotten to put on their numbers.

Look at the runners lining up for the following races.
See if you can work out which ones have forgotten to wear their numbers.

Bronze

1. 78, ☐, 80, ☐, 82, 83, ☐, ☐, 86, ☐

2. 61, ☐, 63, ☐, ☐, 66, 67, ☐, ☐, 70

3. 45, 44, 43, ☐, 41, ☐, 39, 38, ☐, ☐

4. 98, ☐, 96, ☐, ☐, 93, 92, ☐, 90, ☐

5. ☐, 54, 55, ☐, ☐, 58, 59, ☐, 61, ☐

Silver

1. 148, 149, ☐, 151, ☐, ☐, ☐, 154, ☐, 156

2. 197, 198, ☐, ☐, 201, ☐, ☐, 204, ☐

3. 176, 175, 174, ☐, ☐, 171, ☐, ☐, 168

4. 123, ☐, ☐, 126, ☐, 128, ☐, ☐, ☐, 132

5. ☐, 116, ☐, 114, 113, ☐, ☐, 110, ☐

Gold

1. 789, ☐, ☐, 792, ☐, ☐, 795, ☐, ☐

2. 654, ☐, ☐, 651, ☐, ☐, 648, ☐, ☐, 645

3. ☐, ☐, 943, 944, ☐, 946, ☐, ☐, 949, ☐

4. ☐, 499, ☐, ☐, 502, ☐, ☐, ☐, 506,

5. ☐, ☐, ☐, 879, 878, ☐, ☐, ☐, ☐, 873

Training Tips

Read through the sequence after you have finished to make sure it makes sense.

Check first to see if the sequence is going up or down.

Counting in steps of 10

Look at this sequence of numbers:

126, 136, 146, 156, 166, 176, 186, 196, 206...

This sequence goes up in steps of 10.

Which number would come next?　　216

Write the next six numbers in these sequences.

Bronze

Silver

Gold

Bronze	Silver	Gold
1. 30, 40, 50...	1. 70, 80, 90...	1. 743, 753, 763...
2. 100, 90...	2. 130, 120, 110...	2. 328, 318, 308...
3. 56, 66, 76...	3. 89, 99, 109...	3. 974, 964, 954...
4. 43, 53, 63...	4. 134, 144, 154...	4. 469, 479, 489...
5. 98, 88, 78...	5. 86, 96, 106...	5. 935, 925, 915...
6. 7, 17, 27...	6. 133, 123, 113...	6. 276, 286, 296...
7. 35, 45, 55...	7. 135, 145, 155...	7. 821, 811, 801...
8. 60, 70, 80...	8. 37, 47, 57...	8. 102, 112, 122...
9. 111, 101, 91...	9. 122, 112, 102...	9. 557, 567, 577...
10. 72, 82, 92...	10. 61, 71, 81...	10. 940, 930, 920...

Training Tips

When counting in tens, the digit in the units column does not change.

Read the sequences out loud to help you hear the pattern of numbers.

Counting in steps of 100

Look at this sequence of numbers:

256, 356, 456, 556, 656, 756...

This sequence goes up in steps of 100.
Which number would come next? | 856 |

Write the next five numbers in these sequences.

 Bronze

1. 100, 200, 300...

2. 300, 400, 500...

3. 800, 700, 600...

4. 200, 300, 400...

5. 700, 600, 500...

6. 900, 800, 700...

7. 400, 500, 600...

8. 500, 600, 700...

9. 350, 450, 550...

10. 950, 850, 750...

 Silver

1. 126, 226, 326...

2. 250, 350, 450...

3. 974, 874, 774...

4. 980, 880, 780...

5. 348, 448, 548...

6. 835, 735, 635...

7. 702, 602...

8. 313, 413, 513...

9. 528, 628, 728...

10. 931, 831, 731...

 Gold

1. 653, 753...

2. 902, 802...

3. 701, 801...

4. 820, 920...

5. 944, 844...

6. 906, 806...

7. 625, 725...

8. 1133, 1033...

9. 789, 889...

10. 1265, 1165...

 **Training Tips**

 When counting in steps of 100 the tens and units do not change.

 Read the sequences out loud to help you hear the pattern of numbers.

Odd and even numbers

An even number divides exactly by two but an odd number leaves one left over.

Example

Odd number

15

Even number

10

Bronze

a) **Sort these numbers into odd and even:**

24	31	15
22	19	36
7	20	33
13	28	39
40	26	10
5	47	42
37	14	34

b) **Write the next 4 numbers in these strings:**

1. 23, 25, 27...

2. 32, 30, 28...

3. 24, 26, 28...

4. 49, 47, 45...

5. 13, 15, 17...

Silver

a) **List all the even numbers between:**

1. 61 and 73

2. 48 and 36

3. 89 and 104

4. 95 and 83

5. 102 and 115

b) **List all the odd numbers between:**

1. 76 and 89

2. 94 and 78

3. 41 and 53

4. 109 and 97

5. 126 and 113

Gold

a) **Use these digits to make six different three-digit numbers. Then sort them into odd and even numbers. For example, using 3, 4 and 7:**

odd **347 743 473 437**

even **374 734**

1. 2, 4 and 5

2. 7, 5 and 3

3. 8, 1 and 9

4. 6, 4 and 8

5. 8, 7 and 9

b) **Write the next 4 numbers in these strings:**

1. 326, 324, 322...

2. 415, 413, 411...

3. 454, 456, 458...

4. 225, 223, 221...

5. 186, 188, 190...

Training Tips

 Even numbers always end in 0, 2, 4, 6 or 8.

 Odd numbers always end in 1, 3, 5, 7 or 9.

Counting in 3s, 4s and 5s

> **2, 7, 12, 17...**

This pattern goes forward in steps of 5.
The next numbers would be 22, 27, 32, 37, 42...

Look at the patterns below.
For each pattern write the rule to describe the sequence
and write the next five numbers.

 Bronze

1. 0, 3, 6, 9...

2. 5, 10, 15, 20...

3. 16, 14, 12, 10...

4. 4, 8, 12, 16...

5. 9, 12, 15, 18...

6. 27, 24, 21, 18...

7. 75, 70, 65, 60...

8. 29, 27, 25, 23...

9. 12, 16, 20, 24...

10. 2, 5, 8, 11...

 Silver

1. 5, 8, 11, 14...

2. 38, 34, 30, 26...

3. 11, 16, 21, 26...

4. 77, 74, 71, 68...

5. 33, 37, 41, 45...

6. 1, 4, 7, 10...

7. 94, 89, 84, 79...

8. 40, 36, 32, 28...

9. 3, 8, 13, 18...

10. 66, 69, 72, 75...

 Gold

There are some missing numbers to fill in here too.

1. 84, 88, 92...

2. 13, 16, ☐, 22...

3. 124, 119, 114...

4. 117, 113, 109...

5. 69, 66, 63...

6. 83, ☐, 93, 98...

7. 97, ☐, 87, 82...

8. 85, 88, ☐, 94...

9. 64, 68, 72...

10. ☐, 52, 49, 46...

 **Training Tips**

 Look for a pattern in the units.

 Always look at the first two numbers first.

Many multiples

'Multiples' means the same as 'lots of' or 'counting in steps of'.

A multiple of 2 could be 2, 4, 6, 8...

A multiple of 5 could be 5, 10, 15, 20...

Some numbers are multiples of many other numbers.

10 is a multiple of 2, 5 and 10!

Bronze

Use a 100 square. Colour red all the multiples of 2. Colour blue all the multiples of 5. Colour green all the multiples of 10.

1. Which numbers are a multiple of 10?
2. Which numbers are a multiple of 2 and 5?
3. Which numbers are a multiple of 5 only?
4. Which numbers are a multiple of 2, 5 and 10?
5. Look at the multiples of 10. What do you notice about them?

Silver

5	15	22	28	30	35
36	40	45	50	52	55
56	60	65	74	80	88
95	100				

Look at the numbers above.

1. Which are multiples of 10?
2. Which are multiples of 5?
3. Write three multiples of 2.
4. Which are multiples of 10 greater than 36?
5. Which are multiples of 5 less than 56?
6. Which is a multiple of 2 between 35 and 40?
7. Which is a multiple of 2 and 10?
8. Which two are multiples of 2, 5, 8 and 10?

Gold

Use a number line to 30. See if you can find:

1. The multiples of 2, 5 and 10
2. A multiple of 2 and 5 that is greater than 10
3. Two multiples of 3 and 2 that are less than 15
4. The multiples of 5 but not 10
5. A multiple of 4 and 5
6. Three multiples of 2 and 10
7. A multiple of 3 and 5 that comes between 10 and 20
8. All the multiples of 2 and 4

Training Tips

 Multiples of 2 end in 0, 2, 4, 6 or 8.

 Multiples of 5 end in 0 or 5.
Multiples of 10 end in 0.

Reading and writing numbers

It is important to know how to write numbers as words as well as digits.
Here are some words you might find useful:

twenty = 20	thirty = 30	forty = 40	fifty = 50
sixty = 60	seventy = 70	eighty = 80	ninety = 90
hundred = 100	thousand = 1000		

Bronze

a) **Write these words as numbers:**

1. twenty-five
2. forty-seven
3. eighty-three
4. thirty-nine
5. ninety-one

b) **Now write these numbers as words:**

1. 68
2. 76
3. 90
4. 37
5. 16

Silver

a) **Write these words as numbers:**

1. two hundred and thirty
2. four hundred and sixty-three
3. five hundred and seven
4. eight hundred and eleven
5. nine hundred and forty-eight

b) **Now write these numbers as words:**

1. 308
2. 617
3. 150
4. 862
5. 921

Gold

a) **Write these words as numbers:**

1. eight hundred and twelve
2. four hundred and one
3. two thousand, three hundred and seventy
4. five thousand, six hundred and twenty-eight
5. three thousand, eight hundred and ninety-six

b) **Now write these numbers as words:**

1. 2483
2. 6004
3. 1073
4. 6412
5. 7516

Training Tips

 Read the words out loud to help you hear the number.

 Make sure you have written the hundreds, tens and units in the correct places.

Hundreds, tens and units

All three-digit numbers are made up of hundreds, tens and units.
Make sure you read them in that order! This is called **partitioning**.

Example
$356 = 300 + 50 + 6$
Two-digit numbers have just tens and units. $67 = 60 + 7$
Don't forget about zero as a place holder! $106 = 100 + 0 + 6$

Bronze

a) Partition these numbers:

1. 68
2. 91
3. 16
4. 118
5. 113

b) Fill in the missing numbers to make each sum correct:

1. $36 = 30 + \square$
2. $55 = 50 + \square$
3. $90 = \square + 0$
4. $106 = \square + \square + 6$
5. $110 = 100 + \square + \square$

Silver

a) Partition these numbers:

1. 129
2. 630
3. 411
4. 573
5. 702

b) Fill in the missing numbers to make each sum correct:

1. $187 = 100 + \square + 7$
2. $364 = 300 + 60 + \square$
3. $503 = 500 + 0 + \square$
4. $414 = 400 + \square + 4$
5. $910 = 900 + \square + 0$

Gold

a) Partition these numbers:

1. 2538
2. 1049
3. 4950
4. 4444
5. 8009

b) Fill in the missing numbers to make each sum correct:

1. $1726 = 1000 + \square + 20 + 6$
2. $2058 = \square + 0 + 50 + 8$
3. $3947 = 3000 + 900 + \square + 7$
4. $5409 = 5000 + 400 + 0 + \square$
5. $8060 = \square + 0 + 60 + 0$

Training Tips

Remember it is hundreds then tens then units.
Read from left to right just as you would with words.

Hundreds, tens and units - making numbers

The numbers on the judge's scoreboard have all fallen off. The digits are 5, 9 and 6. Using these numbers, there are six different possible scores:

| 569 | 596 | 659 | 695 | 956 | 965 |

The highest possible score would be 965 and the lowest would be 569

Bronze

Using all the digits list all the different possible scores.
Underline the lowest score and put a circle around the highest one.

1. 9 8
2. 5 3
3. 2 7
4. 5 6 4
5. 3 2 1
6. 1 7 6
7. 6 4 2
8. 9 5 1
9. 7 5 3
10. 4 8 6

Silver

Using all the digits list all the different possible scores.
Underline the lowest score and put a circle around the highest one.

1. 2 5 3
2. 9 6 2
3. 1 0 8
4. 7 1 4
5. 8 3 3
6. 4 7 2
7. 6 1 0
8. 3 6 5 4
9. 4 8 8
10. 3 0 7 8

Gold

Write the possible scores in order from lowest to highest:

1. 2 5 9
2. 8 7 6
3. 2 0 3
4. 6 1 1
5. 0 5 7
6. 4 8 5
7. 6 2 6
8. 5 5 7
9. 4 9 6
10. 1 8 0

 Training Tips

 The largest number starts with the highest digit.

 The smallest number starts with the lowest digit.

Finding halfway

In the relay races the second team member has to stand exactly halfway along the track.

If the race was 100 m long the second runner would stand at 50 m.

0 m   50 m   100 m

Draw number lines and mark off the halfway point to show where the runners would start in these races.

Bronze

1. 10 m   *2.* 30 m

3. 50 m   *4.* 100 m

5. 200 m

Silver

1. 150 m   *2.* 200 m

3. 90 m   *4.* 120 m

5. 110 m

Gold

1. 300 m   *2.* 240 m

3. 420 m   *4.* 350 m

5. 430 m

The third runner has to start exactly halfway between the second runner and the end of the race. In these races, find the halfway point between the numbers given to show where the third runner would start.

1. 10 m and 20 m	*1.* 40 m and 60 m	*1.* 200 m and 400 m
2. 25 m and 31 m	*2.* 200 m and 300 m	*2.* 340 m and 350 m
3. 9 m and 13 m	*3.* 80 m and 120 m	*3.* 2000 m and 2100 m
4. 100 m and 200 m	*4.* 300 m and 350 m	*4.* 19 m and 20 m
5. 30 m and 50 m	*5.* 120 m and 130 m	*5.* 3500 m and 3600 m

Training Tips

When finding half of a three-digit number, halve the hundreds and tens separately and then recombine.
Half of 440 is half of 400 + half of 40 = 200 + 20 = 220

Adding 1, 10 or 100... subtracting 1, 10 or 100

In the second round of a darts competition players can score 1, 10 or 100 points.

However, if they miss, they lose 1, 10 or 100 points.

This is shown on the scoreboard as +1, +10, +100 or −1, −10, −100.

Their score starts with their score from the previous round.

For example, player one scored 17 points in Round 1.
Here is the sum for his points in Round 2.

$$17 + 1 - 10 + 10 + 1 + 10 + 1 - 10 + 10 - 10 - 1 = 19$$

Work out the Round 2 scores for these players.

Bronze

1. $28 + 1 + 10 + 10 - 10 - 10 - 10 + 1 + 10 - 1 + 1 = \square$

2. $31 + 10 + 10 - 1 - 10 + 1 + 1 + 10 - 10 - 1 + 10 = \square$

3. $45 + 1 + 1 + 10 + 10 - 1 + 1 - 10 + 10 - 1 - 1 = \square$

4. $29 + 10 + 10 + 1 - 10 - 1 + 10 + 10 - 1 - 10 + 1 = \square$

5. $67 - 1 + 10 + 10 + 1 - 10 - 1 + 10 - 1 - 10 + 1 = \square$

6. $50 - 1 + 10 + 1 + 1 + 10 - 10 + 10 + 1 + 10 - 10 = \square$

7. $43 + 10 - 1 - 1 + 10 - 10 - 1 + 10 + 1 + 1 - 10 = \square$

8. $83 + 10 - 1 - 10 - 1 - 1 + 10 + 10 - 1 + 10 - 1 = \square$

9. $77 + 10 - 1 - 10 + 1 + 10 + 1 - 10 - 1 + 10 + 1 = \square$

Training Tips

 When adding or subtracting 10, the digit in the units column does not change.

 When adding or subtracting 100, the digits in the tens or units columns do not change.

Adding 1, 10 or 100… subtracting 1, 10 or 100

Work out the Round 2 scores for these players.

Silver

1. 86 + 10 −1 − 10 + 1 + 10 + 10 + 1 + 10 − 10 − 1 = ☐

2. 77 − 10 + 1 + 1 + 10 + 10 + 1 + 10 − 1 −1 + 10 = ☐

3. 94 + 10 + 10 − 1 − 1 + 1 − 10 − 10 − 10 + 10 + 1 = ☐

4. 63 − 1 + 100 − 10 + 10 + 1 + 10 − 100 + 10 + 1 + 10 = ☐

5. 146 − 100 + 10 + 10 + 1 − 10 − 1 + 100 + 100 + 1 +10 = ☐

6. 137 + 10 + 1 + 100 − 10 −10 + 100 − 1 − 1 + 100 − 10 = ☐

7. 621 − 100 + 10 + 10 + 1 − 100 −10 + 1 − 1 + 100 + 10 = ☐

8. 321 + 100 − 1 + 10 + 100 + 1 − 10 − 100 + 1 + 10 − 100 = ☐

9. 842 + 100 − 10 −10 + 1 + 100 + 10 − 100 − 1 −1 − 10 = ☐

Gold

1. 851 + 10 − 10 + 100 + 100 − 1 − 10 + 100 + 10 − 1 − 100 = ☐

2. 946 + 100 − 1 + 10 + 100 − 1 − 10 − 100 + 10 − 1 − 100 = ☐

3. 786 + 100 − 1 +100 − 10 + 1 + 100 − 1 − 10 + 100 − 1 = ☐

4. 902 + 100 − 1 + 10 − 1 − 10 − 1 − 100 + 10 + 100 + 1 = ☐

5. 899 + 100 + 1 + 10 −100 − 1 + 10 + 10 + 100 − 1 − 100 = ☐

6. The scores have fallen off the board. After five darts, player 6 has increased his score from 86 to 294. What must he have scored with each of his five darts?

7. After five darts, player 7 has increased his score from 124 to 345. What must he have scored with each of his five darts?

8. After five darts, player 8 has increased her score from 140 to 352. What must she have scored with each of her five darts?

9. After five darts, player 9 has increased her score from 103 to 201. What must she have scored with each of her five darts?

Ordering numbers

For each of these sets, put the numbers in order from highest to lowest.

> For example, in this set the numbers are: 128 224 103 217 147
>
> So, the numbers in order from highest to lowest are: 224 217 147 128 103

Now try these.

Bronze

1. 26 62 94 47 82
2. 63 24 42 36 87
3. 102 95 76 98 84
4. 27 16 85 72 52
5. 46 94 75 35 36
6. 21 95 64 22 59
7. 6 87 65 27 95
8. 50 45 54 51 40

Silver

1. 136 258 285 163 208
2. 108 208 180 218 280
3. 363 316 236 632 216
4. 424 442 451 452 414
5. 951 915 874 847 997
6. 121 212 112 222 201
7. 456 987 746 315 851
8. 964 514 875 231 108

Gold

1. 1875 1234 2971 1006 1946
2. 3214 3987 2014 1056 1579
3. 2145 2864 5142 3647 5974
4. 1069 9601 6901 6019 1961
5. 3412 3241 4123 1234 3214

These sets are in order from lowest to highest.
Some of the numbers are missing.
Make up your own numbers to fill in the blanks.

1. 27 ☐ 54 65 ☐
2. ☐ 45 ☐ ☐ 95
3. ☐ 79 87 ☐ ☐
4. 95 ☐ ☐ 113 ☐
5. 16 ☐ ☐ 24 ☐

1. 125 ☐ ☐ 168 ☐
2. 245 ☐ 254 ☐ ☐
3. ☐ ☐ 147 ☐ 159
4. 369 ☐ 376 ☐ 402
5. ☐ 875 ☐ 987 ☐

1. 1026 ☐ ☐ 1030 ☐
2. 2965 ☐ 3000 ☐ ☐
3. 4736 ☐ ☐ ☐ 5001
4. ☐ ☐ 5478 ☐ 5589
5. ☐ 2147 ☐ ☐ 2156

Training Tips

Look at the *hundreds* then the *tens* then the *units*.

Ordering more numbers

In the swimming competition, the competitors wear numbers generated using the Randomiser machine. When the digits 5, 2 and 7 are inputted into the machine, the possible numbers generated are:

527   572   752   725   257   275

When written in order these become:

257   275   527   572   725   752

Work out all the possible numbers when these digits are put into the machine and write them in order from lowest to highest.

 Bronze

1. | 2 | 5 | 3 |
2. | 6 | 1 | 9 |
3. | 1 | 6 | 8 |
4. | 3 | 7 | 1 |
5. | 8 | 2 | 6 |
6. | 1 | 1 | 5 |
7. | 3 | 0 | 4 |
8. | 8 | 7 | 4 |
9. | 6 | 0 | 3 |
10. | 5 | 5 | 7 |

 Silver

1. | 4 | 5 | 6 |
2. | 7 | 8 | 6 |
3. | 2 | 4 | 3 |
4. | 1 | 1 | 9 |
5. | 0 | 5 | 3 |
6. | 7 | 4 | 6 | 2 |
7. | 3 | 7 | 9 | 0 |
8. | 9 | 9 | 4 |
9. | 1 | 0 | 6 | 7 |
10. | 5 | 5 | 9 | 5 |

 Gold

1. | 1 | 0 | 2 | 3 |
2. | 9 | 6 | 7 | 8 |
3. | 4 | 0 | 5 | 6 |
4. | 6 | 6 | 7 | 7 |
5. | 2 | 5 | 4 | 3 |
6. | 1 | 0 | 3 | 2 |
7. | 8 | 7 | 6 | 8 |
8. | 9 | 9 | 4 | 8 |
9. | 3 | 0 | 6 | 9 |
10. | 5 | 5 | 7 | 5 |

 Training Tips

 When writing numbers in order look at the *hundreds* then the *tens* then the *units*.

Estimating

In the javelin throw, the judges have to estimate how far each contestant has thrown their javelin.

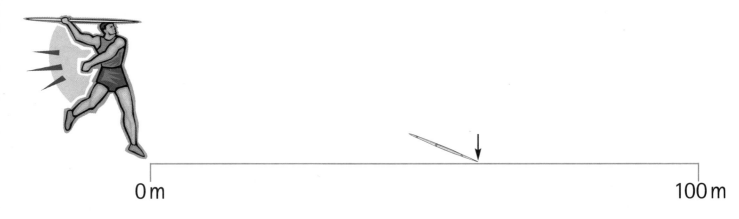

0 m   100 m

This contestant has thrown his javelin approximately 60 m.

Look at each line below and estimate how far each contestant has thrown their javelin.

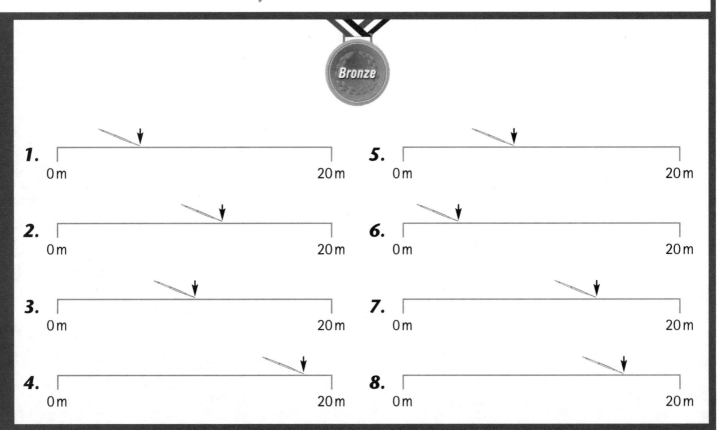

Bronze

1.
0 m   20 m

2.
0 m   20 m

3.
0 m   20 m

4.
0 m   20 m

5.
0 m   20 m

6.
0 m   20 m

7.
0 m   20 m

8.
0 m   20 m

Training Tips

Make sure you check the length of the number line (look at the end point).

Estimating

Look at each line below and estimate how far each
contestant has thrown their javelin.

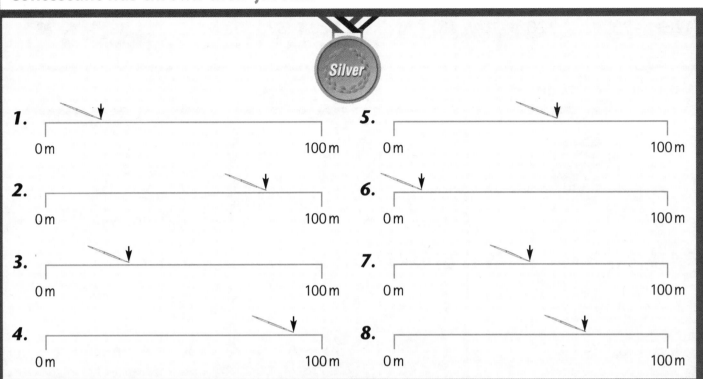

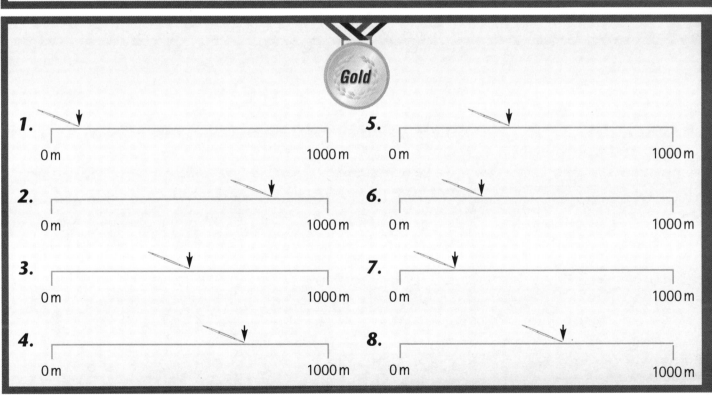

**Training
Tips**

Work out what number would be halfway and decide if the
javelin has gone more than or less than halfway.

Greater than or less than?

Greedy Gordon the crocodile always eats the biggest number.
Make sure his open jaws are pointed towards the highest number.

126 < 473   20 + 10 > 15 + 5   23 < 87 < 93

Complete these using < or >:

Bronze	Silver	Gold
1. 65 * 74	**1.** 265 * 256	**1.** £6.06 * £6.60
2. 96 * 26	**2.** 921 * 931	**2.** 3021 * 3012
3. 43 * 156	**3.** 1000 * 999	**3.** 130 + 70 * 200 − 10
4. 3 + 5 * 6 + 1	**4.** 10 + 28 * 30 + 6	**4.** 50 × 4 * 500 ÷ 2
5. 7 + 5 * 10 − 2	**5.** £7.70 * £ 70.07	**5.** 124 + 29 * 173 − 21

Copy and complete:

1. 26 < ☐	**1.** 100 < ☐ < 200	**1.** 398 < ☐ < 403
2. 72 > ☐	**2.** ☐ < 76 < ☐	**2.** 2197 < ☐ < 2200
3. 10 < ☐ < 20	**3.** 213 < ☐ < 220	**3.** £17.24 < ☐ < £18
4. 52 < ☐ < 90	**4.** ☐ < 1 < ☐	**4.** 4 < ☐ < 5
5. 25 < ☐ < 30	**5.** 420 < ☐ < 430	**5.** 3 × 2 < ☐ < 5 × 3

Training Tips

Make sure the *small* end of the arrow points towards the *smaller* number and the *big* end of the arrow points towards the *bigger* number. Remember the greedy crocodile!

Rounding numbers to nearest 10

In the high jump competition, the height jumped is rounded to the nearest 10 to give each competitor their score.

Example
28 m ➝ 30 points
41 m ➝ 40 points

Round these numbers to the nearest 10 to give the competitors' scores.

 Bronze

1. 51 m
2. 62 m
3. 35 m
4. 99 m
5. 80 m

 Silver

1. 56 m
2. 85 m
3. 123 m
4. 110 m
5. 157 m

 Gold

1. 238 m
2. 109 m
3. 450 m
4. 526 m
5. 675 m

For each of the following scores, list the distances the high jumper could have jumped.

For example, if a competitor scored 70 points she could have jumped:

65 m   66 m   67 m   68 m   69 m   70 m   71 m   72 m   73 m   or 74 m

1. 80	1. 130	1. 350
2. 90	2. 190	2. 740
3. 50	3. 250	3. 900
4. 40	4. 60	4. 630
5. 10	5. 100	5. 770

 **Training Tips**

 If a number ends in 0, 1, 2, 3 or 4 round it down to the nearest 10.

 If a number ends in 5, 6, 7, 8 or 9 round it up to the nearest 10.

Rounding numbers to nearest 100

In the timed cycle race, the distances covered are rounded to the nearest 100.

Example

347 m ⟶ 300 m

486 m ⟶ 500 m

Round each of these distances to the nearest 100.

Bronze	**Silver**	**Gold**
1. 123 m	**1.** 433 m	**1.** 650 m
2. 98 m	**2.** 124 m	**2.** 985 m
3. 146 m	**3.** 350 m	**3.** 261 m
4. 203 m	**4.** 587 m	**4.** 1369 m
5. 165 m	**5.** 730 m	**5.** 1431 m
6. 225 m	**6.** 746 m	**6.** 49 m
7. 190 m	**7.** 25 m	**7.** 901 m
8. 167 m	**8.** 634 m	**8.** 1387 m

List five distances that could be rounded to the following:

1. 100	**1.** 800	**1.** 1200
2. 500	**2.** 500	**2.** 1400
3. 300	**3.** 300	**3.** 1600
4. 200	**4.** 700	**4.** 1100
5. 400	**5.** 200	**5.** 1700

Training Tips

Look at the number of 10s in each number. If there are less than five 10s the number rounds down to 100. If there are five or more then the number rounds up to the next 100.

Fractions of shapes

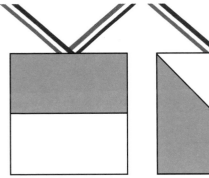

These sports medals are made from regular shapes that have different fractions coloured, for example, a square with $\frac{1}{2}$ coloured.

> **Draw pictures to show each of the following designs. You will need some 2-D shapes to draw around and a ruler to divide the shape into parts.**

Bronze

1. A circle with $\frac{1}{2}$ blue
2. A square with $\frac{1}{2}$ red
3. A rectangle with $\frac{1}{4}$ green
4. A hexagon with one half orange
5. A circle with one quarter purple
6. A diamond with half yellow
7. A square with one quarter pink
8. A triangle with half black
9. A rectangle with half red and $\frac{1}{4}$ orange

Silver

1. A triangle with $\frac{1}{2}$ red
2. A square with $\frac{1}{3}$ orange
3. A rectangle with $\frac{1}{8}$ yellow
4. A rectangle with $\frac{1}{10}$ blue
5. A hexagon with $\frac{1}{2}$ green
6. A diamond with half pink
7. A square with half purple and $\frac{1}{4}$ yellow
8. A circle with $\frac{1}{2}$ red and $\frac{1}{2}$ green
9. An oval with half brown

Gold

1. A rectangle with $\frac{1}{8}$ red and $\frac{1}{8}$ blue
2. A circle with $\frac{1}{2}$ orange and one quarter red
3. A square with $\frac{1}{4}$ yellow and $\frac{1}{2}$ green
4. A circle with $\frac{1}{2}$ blue and $\frac{1}{8}$ orange
5. A square with $\frac{1}{3}$ brown
6. A hexagon with $\frac{1}{6}$ pink
7. A semicircle with $\frac{1}{2}$ green
8. A rectangle with $\frac{1}{10}$ purple and $\frac{1}{2}$ blue
9. A diamond with $\frac{1}{4}$ green and $\frac{1}{4}$ red

Training Tips

 When dividing your shape make sure that all parts are exactly the same.

 When reading fractions make sure you read the top number first.

Equivalent fractions

1							
$\frac{1}{2}$				$\frac{1}{2}$			
$\frac{1}{4}$		$\frac{1}{4}$		$\frac{1}{4}$		$\frac{1}{4}$	
$\frac{1}{8}$	$\frac{1}{8}$	$\frac{1}{8}$	$\frac{1}{8}$	$\frac{1}{8}$	$\frac{1}{8}$	$\frac{1}{8}$	$\frac{1}{8}$

'Equivalent fractions' means two fractions that are the same.

For example $\frac{1}{2}$ is the same as $\frac{2}{4}$.

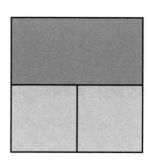

For each of these, draw a square and colour in the fraction shown. Which ones are equivalent fractions?

Bronze

1. $\frac{1}{2}$ 2. $\frac{1}{8}$
3. $\frac{2}{4}$ 4. $\frac{4}{8}$
5. $\frac{1}{4}$ 6. $\frac{4}{4}$
7. $\frac{2}{8}$ 8. $\frac{2}{2}$
9. $\frac{3}{4}$ 10. $\frac{6}{8}$

Silver

1. $\frac{4}{8}$ 2. $\frac{3}{4}$
3. $\frac{1}{2}$ 4. $\frac{2}{2}$
5. $\frac{1}{4}$ 6. $\frac{6}{8}$
7. $\frac{5}{10}$ 8. $\frac{2}{4}$
9. $\frac{8}{8}$ 10. $\frac{2}{8}$

Gold

1. $\frac{5}{10}$ 2. $\frac{3}{4}$
3. $\frac{3}{6}$ 4. $\frac{1}{2}$
5. $\frac{6}{8}$ 6. $\frac{2}{2}$
7. $\frac{1}{4}$ 8. $\frac{2}{6}$
9. $\frac{8}{8}$ 10. $\frac{1}{3}$

Training Tips

The bottom number of the fraction tells you how many parts the shape must be divided into. The top number of the fraction tells you how many parts to colour in.

Fractions of a set

A set of objects can also be divided into fractions.
For example ½ of this set of 10 balls is blue.

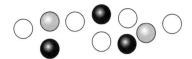

Draw pictures to show the following:

 Bronze

1. 10 cars, one half blue

2. 12 biscuits, ¼ chocolate

3. 8 pencils, ½ red

4. 8 children, one quarter girls

5. 20 flowers, one half pink

6. 16 lorries, one half brown

7. 20 triangles, ¼ orange

8. 14 balls, one half green

9. 4 apples, ¼ green

10. 12 buttons, ½ black

 Silver

1. 10 cars, 1/10 blue

2. 12 biscuits, ⅓ chocolate

3. 28 pencils, ½ red

4. 16 children, ¼ girls

5. 20 flowers, one fifth pink

6. 24 lorries, one quarter brown

7. 20 triangles, one tenth orange

8. 30 balls, one half green

9. 15 apples, one third green

10. 10 buttons, ⅕ brown and ½ black

 Gold

1. 20 cars, one half blue and one quarter red

2. 30 biscuits, ⅓ chocolate

3. 28 pencils, ¼ red and ½ green

4. 20 people, ⅕ children and ¼ women

5. 12 flowers, one half blue and one third pink

6. 15 lorries, ⅕ brown and ⅓ black

7. 10 triangles, one half yellow and one fifth orange

8. 24 balls, ⅓ red and ¼ green

9. 24 apples, one sixth green

10. 12 buttons, ⅓ brown and ¼ blue

 **Training Tips**

 When dividing a set of objects into parts to find a fraction, make sure each part has the same number of objects in it.

Mixed numbers

A mixed number is made from a whole number and a fraction.

$2\frac{1}{2}$ is a mixed number.

On the number line it would be here

```
        ↓
0   1   2   3
```

Look at the following number lines.
For each one write what mixed number is shown and draw pictures of circles to show the number.

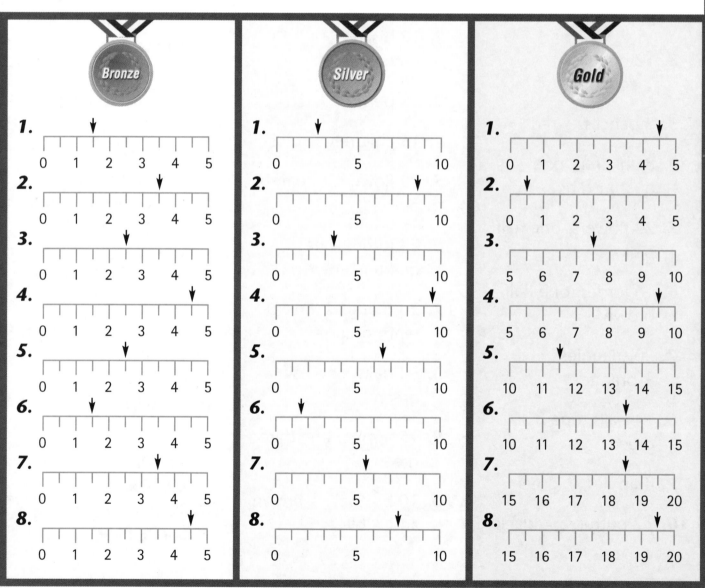

Fraction sequences

Look at this list of numbers:

1   1½   2   2½   ☐   3½   4   4½   5   ☐   6

It contains whole numbers and mixed numbers.

What could the missing numbers be? Where would 5½ and 3 go?

Copy the sequences below and write in the missing fractions.

 Bronze

1. 1 ☐ 2 ☐ 3 ☐ 4 ☐ 5

2. 2 ☐ 3 ☐ 4 ☐ 5 ☐ 6

3. 4 ☐ 5 ☐ 6 ☐ 7 ☐ 8

4. 0 ☐ 1 ☐ 2 ☐ 3 ☐ 4

5. 6 ☐ 7 ☐ 8 ☐ 9 ☐ 10

6. 3 ☐ 4 ☐ 5 ☐ 6 ☐ 7

7. 5 ☐ 6 ☐ 7 ☐ 8 ☐ 9

8. 8 ☐ 9 ☐ 10 ☐ 11 ☐

9. 11 ☐ 12 ☐ 13 ☐ 14

10. 7 ☐ 8 ☐ 9 ☐ 10 ☐

 Silver

1. 2 ☐ 3 ☐ 4 ☐ 5 ☐ 6

2. 0 ☐ 1 ☐ 2 ☐ 3 ☐ 4

3. 6 ☐ 7 ☐ 8 ☐ 9 ☐ 10

4. 4 ☐ 5 ☐ 6 ☐ 7 ☐ 8

5. 10 ☐ 11 ☐ 12 ☐ 13

6. 8 ☐ 9 ☐ 10 ☐ 11 ☐

7. 12 ☐ 13 ☐ 14 ☐ 15

8. 15 ☐ 16 ☐ 17 ☐ 18

9. 9 ☐ 10 ☐ 11 ☐ 12

10. 11 ☐ 12 ☐ 13 ☐ 14

Gold

1. 0 ☐ 1 ☐ 2 ☐ 3 ☐ 4

2. 7 ☐ 8 ☐ 9 ☐ 10 ☐

3. 15 ☐ 16 ☐ 17 ☐ 18

4. 2 ☐ ☐ 3 ☐ ☐ 4

5. 5 ☐ ☐ 6 ☐ ☐ 7

6. 6 ☐ 5 ☐ 4 ☐ 3 ☐ 2

7. 4 ☐ ☐ 5 ☐ ☐ 6

8. 10 ☐ 9 ☐ 8 ☐ 7 ☐

9. 12 ☐ 11 ☐ 10 ☐ 9

10. 8 ☐ ☐ 9 ☐ ☐ 10

 **Training Tips**

 When writing the missing fractions, remember to include the whole number.

 Between 3 and 4 the number must be 3½ not just ½.

Fractions on a number line

Fractions can also be written on a number line.

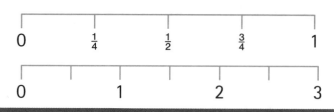

The same works for mixed numbers.
Where would we write $1\frac{1}{2}$ or $2\frac{1}{2}$?

Draw number lines between the numbers given.
Then show the fractions on the number line.
Don't forget to write on all the whole numbers first!

 Bronze

1. 0 to 2. Show $\frac{1}{2}$ and $1\frac{1}{2}$

2. 3 to 5. Show $3\frac{1}{2}$ and $4\frac{1}{2}$

3. 6 to 8. Show $5\frac{1}{2}$ and $6\frac{1}{2}$

4. 7 to 9. Show $7\frac{1}{2}$ and $8\frac{1}{2}$

5. 8 to 10. Show $8\frac{1}{2}$ and $9\frac{1}{2}$

6. 1 to 4. Show $1\frac{1}{2}$ and $3\frac{1}{2}$

7. 4 to 7. Show $4\frac{1}{2}$, $5\frac{1}{2}$ and $6\frac{1}{2}$

8. 5 to 8. Show $6\frac{1}{2}$ and $7\frac{1}{2}$

 Silver

1. 0 to 2. Show $\frac{1}{4}$ and $1\frac{1}{2}$

2. 0 to 3. Show $1\frac{1}{4}$, $1\frac{1}{2}$ and $2\frac{1}{4}$

3. 1 to 4. Show $1\frac{1}{4}$, $2\frac{1}{4}$ and $2\frac{1}{2}$

4. 2 to 5. Show $2\frac{1}{2}$, $3\frac{1}{4}$ and $4\frac{1}{4}$

5. 2 to 6. Show $3\frac{1}{4}$, $3\frac{1}{2}$ and $5\frac{1}{2}$

6. 3 to 6. Show $3\frac{1}{2}$, $4\frac{1}{4}$ and $5\frac{1}{2}$

7. 1 to 4. Show $1\frac{1}{4}$, $1\frac{1}{2}$, and $3\frac{1}{2}$

8. 5 to 8. Show $5\frac{1}{2}$, $6\frac{1}{4}$ and $6\frac{1}{2}$

 Gold

1. 0 to 3. Show $\frac{1}{4}$, $1\frac{1}{2}$ and $2\frac{1}{4}$

2. 2 to 5. Show $2\frac{1}{4}$, $2\frac{3}{4}$ and $4\frac{1}{2}$

3. 4 to 7. Show $4\frac{1}{2}$, $5\frac{1}{4}$ and $6\frac{3}{4}$

4. 5 to 8. Show $5\frac{1}{4}$, $6\frac{3}{4}$ and $7\frac{1}{2}$

5. 6 to 9. Show $6\frac{1}{4}$, $6\frac{3}{4}$, $7\frac{1}{2}$ and $7\frac{3}{4}$

6. 0 to 4. Show $\frac{1}{3}$, $2\frac{1}{3}$ and $3\frac{1}{3}$

7. 1 to 4. Show $1\frac{2}{3}$, $2\frac{1}{3}$ and $2\frac{2}{3}$

8. 5 to 8. Show $5\frac{1}{3}$, $5\frac{2}{3}$, $7\frac{1}{3}$ and $7\frac{2}{3}$

 **Training Tips**

 To find the position on the number line, look at the whole number first.

- $\frac{1}{2}$ is bigger than $\frac{1}{4}$
- $\frac{3}{4}$ is bigger than $\frac{1}{2}$

Learning the vocabulary

There are lots of different ways to say 25 + 15 = 40

The sum of 25 and 15 is 40.
25 plus 15 makes 40.
40 take away 15 leaves 25.
The difference between 40 and 15 is 25.

Word Bank

Add	plus	and	sum of
	How many more is... than...		
Total	altogether		
Minus	How many less is... than...		
	subtract	difference between	
	take away	less	

Use the Word Bank to write these sums using different vocabulary.

 Bronze

1. 15 + 7 =

2. 25 − 6 =

3. 12 − 7 =

4. 20 + 6 =

5. 16 + 8 =

6. 19 − 11 =

7. 20 + 0 =

8. 25 − 3 =

9. 17 − 0 =

10. 12 + 9 =

 Silver

1. 26 + 8 =

2. 21 − 9 =

3. 35 + 3 =

4. 42 − 10 =

5. 27 + 9 =

6. 37 − 20 =

7. 9 + 17 =

8. 24 + 12 =

9. 39 − 7 =

10. 41 − 8 =

 Gold

1. 59 + 7 =

2. 60 − 24 =

3. 37 − 15 =

4. 76 + 124 =

5. 11 + 56 =

6. 36 + 50 =

7. 287 − 22 =

8. 98 − 65 =

9. 212 + 64 =

10. 90 − 45 =

 Olympic Tips

Addition can be done in any order (but it is easier to start with the biggest number).
This doesn't work with subtraction – try it and see!

Using the vocabulary

Use what you learned on page 31 to try these – read carefully!

 **Bronze**

1. 27 add 10 makes ☐

2. 4 plus 18 makes ☐

3. The difference between 17 and 6 is ☐

4. Which two numbers could have a sum of 20?

5. What must I add to 14 to make 19?

6. How many are 10 and 3 altogether?

7. 17 minus 11 leaves ☐

8. Add 12 to 6.

9. How many more is 10 than 4?

10. The total of 16 and 5 is ☐

 Silver

1. 60 plus 40 is ☐

2. What is the total of 18 and 27?

3. What must I add to 19 to make 30?

4. The difference between 18 and 3 is ☐

5. How many are 12 and 37 altogether?

6. How many more is 25 than 16?

7. 23 minus 10 leaves ☐

8. 30 subtract 15 is ☐

9. How many less is 14 than 22?

10. The total of 12 and 13 is ☐

 Gold

1. The difference between 75 and 30 is ☐

2. How many are 21 and 35 altogether?

3. The sum of 17 and 23 is ☐

4. 46 minus 15 leaves ☐

5. What must I add to 40 to make 97?

6. How many less is 17 than 50?

7. Which two numbers have a sum of 37?

8. How many more is 56 than 21?

9. What is the total of 45 and 31?

10. Add 60 to 14.

 **Training Tips**

 Subtraction is the opposite of addition so use this to check your answers.

Number bonds

Sums are much easier to solve if you know all your number bonds – all those addition and subtraction facts for numbers up to 20... 50... even 100!

See how quickly you can do these.
Try them again and see if you can beat your time!
Ready... steady... go!

 Bronze

1. 11 + 4 =

2. 20 − 6 =

3. 16 − 7 =

4. 10 + 9 =

5. 12 + 7 =

6. 19 − 11 =

7. 17 − 4 =

8. 13 + 7 =

9. 8 + 7 =

10. 9 + 8 =

 Silver

1. 26 + 4 =

2. 19 + 7 =

3. 30 − 6 =

4. 21 + 8 =

5. 36 − 4 =

6. 6 + 19 =

7. 15 − 8 =

8. 30 + 0 =

9. 23 − 6 =

10. 15 + 10 =

 Gold

1. 50 + 18 =

2. 25 + 12 =

3. 30 − 15 =

4. 25 + 75 =

5. 55 + 45 =

6. 18 + 22 =

7. 40 − 15 =

8. 35 − 20 =

9. 55 + 30 =

10. 90 − 60 =

 **Training Tips**

Addition can be done in any order (but it is easier to start with the biggest number).
This doesn't work with subtraction – try it and see!

Making 100.. making 1000

It is also useful to know which pairs of numbers make 100 or 1000.

Fill in the blanks to complete these sums.

 Bronze

1. 60 + 40 = ☐
2. 20 + 80 = ☐
3. 0 + ☐ = 100
4. 50 + ☐ = 100
5. ☐ + 90 = 100
6. 70 + ☐ = 100
7. 90 + 10 = ☐
8. ☐ + ☐ = 100
9. ☐ + ☐ = 100
10. ☐ + ☐ = 100

 Silver

1. 65 + 35 = ☐
2. 5 + ☐ = 100
3. 45 + ☐ = 100
4. ☐ + 75 = 100
5. ☐ + 85 = 100
6. 200 + 800 = ☐
7. 900 + ☐ = 1000
8. ☐ + ☐ = 100
9. ☐ + ☐ = 100
10. ☐ + ☐ = 1000

 Gold

1. 700 + ☐ = 1000
2. 200 + ☐ = 1000
3. 50 + ☐ = 1000
4. 650 + 350 = ☐
5. 450 + ☐ = 1000
6. 100 + ☐ = 1000
7. ☐ + 850 = 1000
8. ☐ + ☐ = 1000
9. ☐ + ☐ = 1000
10. ☐ + ☐ = 1000

 **Training Tips**

 Use your number bonds to 10 to help you. 3 + 7 = 10 so 30 + 70 = 100

 Subtraction is the opposite of addition so use this to check your answers.

Adding lots of numbers

Now that you have had lots of practice you are ready to add more than two numbers together. To make this easier, remember addition can be done in any order so start with the biggest number. Then look to see if there are any pairs that make 10 or a multiple of 10.

Here goes...

6 + 17 + 4 = ...Let's rewrite that with the biggest number first.

17 + 6 + 4 = ...Ah! 6 + 4 makes 10 so that leaves

17 + 10   ...the answer must be 27!

It is a good idea to check by adding the numbers together one at a time.

6 + 17 is 23. 23 + 4 is 27 so the answer must be 27.

Try these.
Remember to put the biggest number first and look for pairs that you know.

Bronze

1. 5 + 2 + 13 =

2. 6 + 8 + 4 =

3. 12 + 9 + 8 =

4. 7 + 8 + 3 =

5. 15 + 7 + 5 =

6. 2 + 19 + 1 =

7. 7 + 4 + 2 =

8. 16 + 0 + 4 =

9. 7 + 5 + 3 =

10. 1 + 6 + 9 =

Silver

1. 7 + 5 + 9 =

2. 13 + 8 + 7=

3. 12 + 13 + 3 =

4. 17 + 11 + 3 =

5. 8 + 15 + 2 + 3 =

6. 15 + 7 + 10 + 5 =

7. 1 + 8 + 19 + 5 =

8. 16 + 9 + 14 + 3 =

9. 3 + 5 + 27 + 1 =

10. 9 + 21 + 6 + 4 =

Gold

1. 21 + 8 + 9 + 14 =

2. 7 + 12 + 9 =

3. 9 + 21 + 6 + 4 =

4. 17 + 8+ 13 + 4 =

5. 25 + 6 + 15 + 2 =

6. 3 + 18 + 7 + 6 =

7. 3 + 5 + 21+ 1=

8. 36 + 7 + 14 + 13 =

9. 8 + 19 + 12 +11 =

10. 26 + 7 + 4 + 9 =

 Training Tips

Learn your number bonds to 10 and 20.

 Check your answers by doing the sum again to make sure you get the same answer.

Doubles and near doubles

In the rugby competition, the final scores for each country were calculated by doubling the points scored.

For example, Italy scored 16 so their final score was 32.

Work out the final score for each of these countries.

 Bronze

1. Japan 12

2. Norway 7

3. England 8

4. France 11

5. Spain 10

 Silver

1. Australia 15

2. Scotland 17

3. Ireland 20

4. Switzerland 30

5. Greece 16

 Gold

1. Holland 24

2. Canada 60

3. Hong Kong 19

4. Austria 27

5. Wales 42

Learning doubles off by heart can help you work out answers to 'near doubles'.

For example, 16 + 17 is nearly a double. It is double 16, add one more.
So 16 + 17 = 32 + 1 = 33

Work out these near doubles.

1. 12 + 13 =

2. 7 + 6 =

3. 8 + 9 =

4. 11 + 12 =

5. 10 + 11 =

1. 15 + 16 =

2. 17 + 16 =

3. 20 + 21 =

4. 30 + 29 =

5. 16 + 17 =

1. 24 + 25 =

2. 60 + 70 =

3. 19 + 18 =

4. 27 + 28 =

5. 42 + 43 =

 **Training Tips**

 Doubling means adding two numbers the same together. So double 7 is just 7+7.

 Use your knowledge of doubles to quickly work out near doubles.

Addition and subtraction patterns

Looking for patterns can help turn difficult sums into easy ones!

13 + 5 = 18 so...	79 − 4 = 75 so...	8 + 6 = 14 so...
13 + 15 = 28	79 − 14 = 65	80 + 60 = 140
13 + 25 = 38	79 − 24 = 55	800 + 600 = 1400
13 + 35 = 48	79 − 34 = 45	8000 + 6000 = 14000

Complete these sums. Look at the patterns.

 Bronze

1. 14 + 5 =
24 + 5 =
2. 87 − 3 =
87 − 13 =
3. 2 + 5 =
20 + 50 =
4. 95 − 4 =
95 − 14 =
5. 11 + 8 =
21 + 8 =

 Silver

1. 18 + 16 =
18 + 26 =
2. 19 + 4 =
190 + 40 =
3. 74 − 9 =
74 − 19 =
4. 7 + 16 =
70 + 160 =
5. 99 − 12 =
99 − 22 =

Gold

1. 15 + 16 =
150 + 160 =
2. 119 + 14 =
119 + 24 =
3. 256 − 9 =
256 − 19 =
4. 208 − 103 =
208 − 113 =
5. 17 + 12 =
170 + 120 =

Once you know one fact it is easy to work out three others!

16 + 12 = 28 so...	12 + 16 = 28
28 − 16 = 12	28 − 12 = 16

Write four number sentences for each set of numbers.
Make sure they are correct!

1.	12	7	19	*1.*	24	13	37	*1.*	4	91	87
2.	13	8	21	*2.*	29	16	13	*2.*	23	56	79

 **Training Tips**

 Become a pattern spotter! Use answers to simple sums to work out more difficult ones by following the pattern.

Adding 9 or 11

Adding 9 or 11 to a number is easy if you add 10 first.
Remember 11 = 10 + 1 and 9 = 10 − 1

58 + 9 = 58 + 10 − 1 = 68 − 1 = 67

74 + 11 = 74 + 10 + 1 = 84 + 1 = 85

The same rule applies for adding 19, 29, 39... 21, 31, 41...

64 + 19 = 64 + 20 − 1 = 84 − 1 = 83

95 + 31 = 95 + 30 + 1 = 125 + 1 = 126

Try these sums:

 Bronze

1. 38 + 11 =
2. 44 + 9 =
3. 27 + 21 =
4. 19 + 11 =
5. 24 + 19 =
6. 53 + 21 =
7. 47 + 19 =
8. 41 + 9 =
9. 20 + 19 =
10. 16 + 11 =

 Silver

1. 48 + 39 =
2. 46 + 29 =
3. 63 + 31 =
4. 29 + 59 =
5. 46 + 31 =
6. 58 + 21 =
7. 84 + 31 =
8. 69 + 39 =
9. 76 + 31 =
10. 17 + 71 =

 Gold

1. 428 + 61 =
2. 347 + 69 =
3. 632 + 89 =
4. 479 + 59 =
5. 631 + 51 =
6. 781 + 61 =
7. 258 + 79 =
8. 697 + 81 =
9. 647 + 89 =
10. 369 + 91 =

 Training Tips

 If you are adding 9, take away 1 from the 10.

 If you are adding 11, add 1 to the 10.

alculations **39**

Subtracting 9 or 11

The same rule applies when **subtracting** 9 or 11.
But when you **subtract** 11 remember to −10 then −1
and when you subtract 9, −10 but then +1 back on.

Let's have a look...

$$73 - 11 = 73 - 10 - 1 = 63 - 1 = 62$$

$$61 - 9 = 61 - 10 + 1 = 51 + 1 = 52$$

Try these sums:

Bronze	Silver	Gold
1. 37 − 9 =	**1.** 75 − 51 =	**1.** 214 − 59 =
2. 41 − 11 =	**2.** 54 − 41 =	**2.** 263 − 79 =
3. 54 − 9 =	**3.** 60 − 39 =	**3.** 125 − 89 =
4. 39 − 11 =	**4.** 99 − 59 =	**4.** 136 − 61 =
5. 40 − 9 =	**5.** 47 − 41 =	**5.** 547 − 51 =
6. 37 − 11 =	**6.** 98 − 79 =	**6.** 321 − 91 =
7. 48 − 11 =	**7.** 75 − 69 =	**7.** 236 − 59 =
8. 32 − 19 =	**8.** 284 − 11 =	**8.** 148 − 99 =
9. 24 − 9 =	**9.** 241 − 9 =	**9.** 263 − 41 =
10. 57 − 19 =	**10.** 145 − 31 =	**10.** 411 − 51 =

Training Tips

If you are subtracting 9, add **1** to the 10.

If you are subtracting 11, take away **1** from the 10.

Addition by partitioning

When adding two-digit numbers together, sometimes it is easier
to break them down into their hundreds, tens and units.

Example

$61 + 38 = 60 + 1 + 30 + 8$
$ = 90 + 9$
$ = 99$

$256 + 133 = 200 + 50 + 6 + 100 + 30 + 3$
$ = 300 + 80 + 9$
$ = 389$

Choose two numbers from below and add them together.
Which numbers do you need to use to make the biggest total?
What about the smallest total?

Bronze			
31	16	24	30
52	45	11	32
25	41	33	14
22	43	15	

Silver		
71	56	108
49	224	92
364	88	390
57	125	65
47	69	84
167		

Gold		
256	479	539
219	364	506
424	169	373
106	453	347

Training Tips

 Make sure you add hundreds to hundreds and tens to tens.

Drawing number lines for addition problems

Number lines are a great tool for working out difficult addition sums.

Let's try 87 + 46 =

46 is made up of 4 tens and 6 units so that is what must be added onto 87.

So 87 + 46 = 133

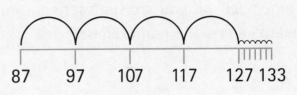

87   97   107   117   127 133

The same can be done for three-digit numbers.

254 + 431 =

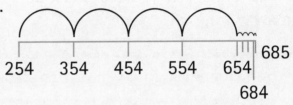

254   354   454   554   654   685

684

Draw number lines to help you work out the following:

Bronze

1. 26 + 13 =

2. 31 + 24 =

3. 40 + 35 =

4. 46 + 22 =

5. 38 + 31 =

6. 54 + 34 =

7. 29 + 41 =

8. 61 + 33 =

9. 74 + 25 =

10. 56 + 43 =

Silver

1. 45 + 37 =

2. 67 + 24 =

3. 53 + 39 =

4. 86 + 42 =

5. 76 + 32 =

6. 84 + 53 =

7. 92 + 87 =

8. 106 + 57 =

9. 124 + 63 =

10. 149 + 26 =

Gold

1. 256 + 104 =

2. 128 + 248 =

3. 369 + 124 =

4. 401 + 258 =

5. 307 + 234 =

6. 428 + 115 =

7. 117 + 209 =

8. 356 + 487 =

9. 294 + 631 =

10. 497 + 501 =

Training Tips

 Start with the biggest number and add on the smallest number.

 Add on the hundreds first, then the tens then the units.

Drawing number lines for subtraction problems

Number lines are also a useful tool for working out subtraction problems. They are drawn exactly the same as for addition.
But remember – if you are subtracting a number you must go backwards along the number line.

Example

86 − 41 =

41 is 4 tens and 1 unit so that must be taken away from 86.

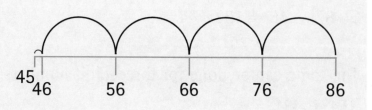

45
46   56   66   76   86

Draw number lines to work out these subtraction sums.

 Bronze

1. 56 − 31 =

2. 62 − 40 =

3. 75 − 32 =

4. 48 − 37 =

5. 39 − 26 =

6. 55 − 44 =

7. 41 − 21 =

8. 79 − 45 =

9. 88 − 63 =

10. 97 − 64 =

 Silver

1. 76 − 58 =

2. 85 − 34 =

3. 54 − 39 =

4. 97 − 61 =

5. 92 − 68 =

6. 72 − 49 =

7. 65 − 58 =

8. 170 − 38 =

9. 155 − 41 =

10. 129 − 18 =

 Gold

1. 456 − 321 =

2. 748 − 326 =

3. 953 − 431 =

4. 631 − 428 =

5. 557 − 296 =

6. 684 − 493 =

7. 721 − 583 =

8. 507 − 329 =

9. 417 − 256 =

10. 624 − 409 =

Training Tips

With subtraction the number gets smaller so check your answers!

Finding the difference between two numbers

If you are asked to find the difference between two numbers, the numbers can be in any order.

Number lines are a really useful tool for working out differences.

Example

To find the difference between 15 and 38 you can use a number line.
The total between the numbers is 23.

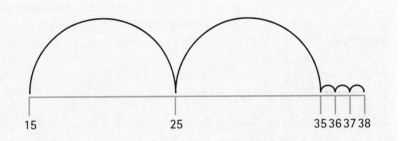

15   25   35 36 37 38

What is the difference between these numbers?

 Bronze

1. 12 and 28
2. 20 and 39
3. 5 and 27
4. 13 and 48
5. 28 and 39

 Silver

1. 38 and 72
2. 41 and 90
3. 27 and 84
4. 39 and 61
5. 40 and 87

 Gold

1. 127 and 183
2. 205 and 279
3. 190 and 263
4. 451 and 281
5. 380 and 651

You can even work some of them out in your head by counting up.
It doesn't matter what order the numbers are in.

Try these without using number lines!

1. 28 and 34
2. 17 and 22
3. 25 and 29
4. 30 and 37
5. 45 and 51

1. 82 and 79
2. 98 and 105
3. 67 and 75
4. 79 and 94
5. 71 and 62

1. 365 and 372
2. 496 and 508
3. 764 and 751
4. 592 and 607
5. 801 and 789

 **Training Tips**

 It doesn't matter what order the numbers are in.
The difference between 45 and 21 is the same as the difference between 21 and 45.

Missing numbers

Sometimes the answer you need is not at the end of the sum but somewhere in the middle.
Drawing a number line can be a useful way of working these out.

Example

26 + ☐ = 42

You need to find the difference between 26 and 42.
The number line shows that the missing number is 16.

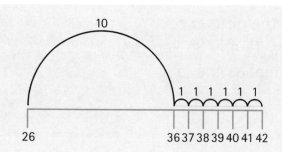

Draw number lines to work out these missing numbers.

 Bronze

1. 16 + ☐ = 27

2. 15 + ☐ = 30

3. 7 + ☐ = 21

4. 24 + ☐ = 46

5. 20 + ☐ = 48

6. 33 + ☐ = 50

7. 12 + ☐ = 31

8. ☐ + 18 = 37

9. ☐ + 15 = 30

10. 29 + ☐ = 47

 Silver

1. 26 + ☐ = 78

2. 34 + ☐ = 59

3. 67 + ☐ = 90

4. 53 + ☐ = 71

5. ☐ + 17 = 45

6. 39 + ☐ = 87

7. 24 + ☐ = 72

8. ☐ + 34 = 47

9. 19 + ☐ = 50

10. ☐ + 28 = 41

 Gold

1. 146 + ☐ = 265

2. 78 + ☐ = 341

3. 211 + ☐ = 580

4. 109 + ☐ = 487

5. ☐ + 346 = 561

6. ☐ + 201 = 741

7. 456 + ☐ = 987

8. 231 + ☐ = 403

9. ☐ + 268 = 340

10. 394 + ☐ = 409

 Training Tips

 Add on any jumps of ten before you add on the units.

 You can check your answers by doing a subtraction sum.

More missing numbers (subtraction)

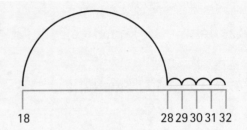

We have already looked at missing numbers in addition sums, but what about subtraction?
Number lines are still a great way to help you out!

Let's look...

☐ − 14 = 18

What number take away 14 leaves 18?

The jumps show what has been taken away so the starting number must have been 32.

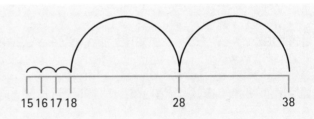

18   28 29 30 31 32

Another one...

38 − ☐ = 15

What must be taken away from 38 to leave 15?

23 needs to be taken away from 38 to leave 15.

15 16 17 18   28   38

Fill in the missing numbers in these sums:

Bronze

1. 25 − ☐ = 16

2. ☐ − 12 = 19

3. 30 − ☐ = 14

4. 28 − ☐ = 7

5. ☐ − 22 = 42

6. ☐ − 18 = 31

7. 49 − ☐ = 31

8. 37 − ☐ = 10

9. ☐ − 31 = 6

10. 50 − ☐ = 25

Silver

1. 65 − ☐ = 42

2. ☐ − 15 = 71

3. ☐ − 21 = 68

4. 81 − ☐ = 64

5. 72 − ☐ = 36

6. ☐ − 18 = 39

7. 59 − ☐ = 41

8. 91 − ☐ = 60

9. ☐ − 16 = 74

10. 100 − ☐ = 55

Gold

1. 275 − ☐ = 204

2. ☐ − 121 = 357

3. ☐ − 187 = 561

4. 844 − ☐ = 590

5. ☐ − 284 = 711

6. 701 − ☐ = 594

7. 579 − ☐ = 162

8. ☐ − 105 = 891

9. ☐ − 361 = 401

10. 946 − ☐ = 689

Training Tips

 Remember to check your answers by working out the subtraction sum.

Putting it into practice

In the cricket competition, the countries scored the following points:

Japan	12	Norway	7	England	8	France	11	Spain	10
Switzerland	35	America	20	Turkey	13	Denmark	14	Russia	6
Iceland	17	Australia	45	Scotland	60	Ireland	20	Greece	36
Finland	25	China	79	Hong Kong	198	Egypt	58	Morocco	80
Germany	63	Holland	324	Canada	160	South Africa	245	Austria	270
Wales	400	Poland	651	Mexico	300	Sweden	500	Brazil	495

Use these scores to answer the following questions:

Bronze

1. How much did Norway and Finland score altogether?

2. What is the difference in score between England and Egypt?

3. How much more did Scotland score than Russia?

4. What is the total of the scores from England and Morocco?

5. How much did Sweden and Russia score altogether?

6. What is the total of the scores from Scotland and Iceland?

7. What is the total of the scores from Morocco and Greece?

8. How much more did China score than Denmark?

9. What is the sum of the scores from Spain and Australia?

10. What is the difference in score between Morocco and Ireland?

Training Tips

Write down the sum if you can't work it out in your head.

Start with the biggest number if you are adding.

Putting it into practice

Use the scores opposite to answer the following questions:

Silver

1. How much did Norway and Holland score altogether?

2. What is the difference in score between South Africa and England?

3. How much more did Wales score than Russia?

4. What is the total of the scores from Germany and Mexico?

5. How much did Morocco and Switzerland score altogether?

6. What is the total of the scores from Greece and Turkey?

7. What is the difference in score between Germany and Finland?

8. How much more did China score than Denmark?

9. What is the sum of the scores from Spain and Brazil?

10. What is the difference in score between Morocco and Canada?

Gold

1. How much did Scotland and Poland score altogether?

2. What is the difference in score between Hong Kong and Greece?

3. How much more did Wales score than South Africa?

4. What is the total of the scores from Poland and Sweden?

5. How much did Canada and Holland score altogether?

6. What is the total of the scores from China and Egypt?

7. What is the difference in score between South Africa and Mexico?

8. How much more did Hong Kong score than France?

9. What is the sum of the scores from Wales, Sweden and Mexico?

10. What is the difference in score between Morocco and South Africa?

Training Tips

Drawing a number line may help.

Break the numbers down into hundreds, tens and units to help you.

Missing hundreds, tens and units

$2 \bullet + \bullet 5 = 56$

What digits do ● represent?

To make 6 we need 1 + 5

To make 50 we need 20 + 30

So the sum should read 21 + 35 = 56

Look at the units, tens and hundreds and try to work out what parts of the sum are missing.

Bronze	Silver	Gold
1. 3 ● + ● 1 = 49	**1.** ● 6 + 2 ● = 47	**1.** 7 ● + ● 3 = 97
2. ● 2 + 4 ● = 62	**2.** 3 ● + ● 5 = 75	**2.** 1 ● + ● 7 = 52
3. 1 ● + ● 2 = 29	**3.** 1 ● + ● 4 = 30	**3.** 3 ● 4 + ● 5 ● = 679
4. 2 ● + ● 3 = 59	**4.** 1 ● + ● 7 = 32	**4.** 2 ● 1 + ● 7 ● = 485
5. ● 1 + 6 ● = 93	**5.** ● 6 + 1 ● = 89	**5.** ● 3 ● + 4 ● 9 = 859
6. ● 6 + 2 ● = 47	**6.** 7 ● − ● 4 = 45	**6.** 8 ● − ● 1 = 35
7. 4 ● + 5 ● = 99	**7.** 8 ● − ● 2 = 17	**7.** ● 4 − 3 ● = 42
8. 3 ● + ● 5 = 75	**8.** ● 8 − 2 ● = 71	**8.** 3 ● 2 − ● 4 ● = 230
9. 1 ● + ● 4 = 30	**9.** ● 3 + 4 ● = 80	**9.** 7 ● 9 − ● 3 ● = 555
10. ● 4 + 3 ● = 58	**10.** ● 8 + 5 ● = 84	**10.** 8 ● + ● 6 = 125

Training Tips

Work out the units, then the tens and then the hundreds.

Try the completed sum to check you get the right answer.

Understanding multiplication

Sports Shop Price List

T-shirts	£4	Sweatshirts	£8	Cap	£5
Tracksuit	£10	Football	£3	Bat	£7
Gloves	£6	Badge	£1	Socks	£2

Work out how much it would cost to buy these items from the sports shop. Write each one as a multiplication sum.
For example, 5 footballs is 5 × £3 = £15

Bronze

1. 4 pairs of socks

2. 3 caps

3. 2 tracksuits

4. 4 badges

5. 2 T-shirts

Silver

1. 4 T-shirts

2. 8 footballs

3. 10 pairs of socks

4. 7 tracksuits

5. 3 sweatshirts

Gold

1. 5 sweatshirts

2. 3 bats

3. 6 pairs of gloves

4. 13 tracksuits

5. 20 pairs of socks

Work out how many of the following you could buy with £20.

1. tracksuits
2. caps
3. socks
4. badges
5. footballs

1. T-shirts
2. footballs
3. sweatshirts
4. caps
5. gloves

1. footballs
2. T-shirts
3. caps and socks
4. footballs and bats
5. badges and gloves

Training Tips

Multiplication is the same as repeated addition.
So 5 × 3 = 3 + 3 + 3 + 3 + 3 = 15

Multiplication facts

See how quickly you can answer these multiplication facts.
Try to learn them.

Bronze

1. 2 × 2 =

2. 3 × 10 =

3. 2 × 10 =

4. 7 × 2 =

5. 4 × 2 =

6. 10 × 10 =

7. 1 × 10 =

8. 2 × 1 =

Silver

1. 10 × 5 =

2. 3 × 3 =

3. 2 × 10 =

4. 4 × 5 =

5. 2 × 8 =

6. 7 × 10 =

7. 10 × 10 =

8. 9 × 2 =

Gold

1. 6 × 3 =

2. 10 × 7 =

3. 12 × 2 =

4. 9 × 3 =

5. 11 × 10 =

6. 0 × 3 =

7. 8 × 4 =

8. 7 × 5 =

Use the facts you know to work out the missing numbers.

1. 3 × ☐ = 6

2. 4 × ☐ = 40

3. 7 × ☐ = 14

4. ☐ × 10 = 60

5. 8 × ☐ = 80

6. ☐ × 2 = 18

7. ☐ × 10 = 100

8. 1 × ☐ = 2

1. 4 × ☐ = 20

2. ☐ × 10 = 90

3. ☐ × 2 = 18

4. 3 × ☐ = 9

5. 10 × ☐ = 0

6. ☐ × 5 = 30

7. 9 × ☐ = 45

8. 10 × ☐ = 100

1. 9 × ☐ = 45

2. 10 × ☐ = 10

3. 8 × ☐ = 32

4. ☐ × 9 = 27

5. 2 × ☐ = 24

6. 4 × ☐ = 36

7. 5 × ☐ = 55

8. ☐ × 10 = 110

Training Tips

 A whole number multiplied by 10 always ends in zero.

 A whole number multiplied by 2 is always even.

Division by grouping

Different sports need teams of different sizes. The coaches need to work out how many teams there will be for each sport.

For example, 20 people in groups of four makes five teams. Look at the picture.

Can you work out how many teams there will be for each sport?

Bronze

1. Hockey – 12 people in groups of 3

2. Table tennis – 16 people in groups of 4

3. Long jump – 10 people in groups of 5

4. Rugby – 18 people in groups of 9

5. Darts – 8 people in groups of 2

6. Table football – 12 people in groups of 4

7. Javelin – 15 people in groups of 3

8. Gymnastics – 20 people in groups of 5

Silver

1. Long jump – 20 people in teams of 4

2. Relay running – 18 people in teams of 3

3. Swimming – 35 people in teams of 5

4. Badminton – 24 people in teams of 4

5. Squash – 32 people in teams of 4

6. High jump – 22 people in teams of 2

7. Football – 44 people in teams of 11

8. Karate – 20 people in teams of 5

Gold

1. Tennis – 36 people in teams of 4

2. Judo – 45 people in teams of 5

3. Rugby – 54 people in teams of 9

4. Discus – 27 people in teams of 3

5. Rowing – 44 people in teams of 4

6. Relay races – 65 people in teams of 5

7. Triple jump – 30 people in teams of 6

8. Netball – 36 people in teams of 4

Training Tips

Division is the same as repeated subtraction.
20 ÷ 4 is 20 – 4 – 4 – 4 – 4 – 4.
So 20 ÷ 4 = 5 (5 lots of 4)

Division by sharing

Another way of dividing is by sharing.

Example

12 ÷ 3   12 shared between 3 is 4 each.

Work out how many medals each person in the team gets when the total is shared out equally among them.

Bronze	Silver	Gold
1. 16 ÷ 4 =	**1.** 30 ÷ 6 =	**1.** 44 ÷ 4 =
2. 15 ÷ 3 =	**2.** 40 ÷ 4 =	**2.** 65 ÷ 5 =
3. 20 ÷ 2 =	**3.** 27 ÷ 3 =	**3.** 120 ÷ 10 =
4. 9 ÷ 3 =	**4.** 35 ÷ 5 =	**4.** 32 ÷ 4 =
5. 10 ÷ 5 =	**5.** 24 ÷ 2 =	**5.** 36 ÷ 3 =
6. 18 ÷ 2 =	**6.** 24 ÷ 6 =	**6.** 45 ÷ 5 =
7. 20 ÷ 4 =	**7.** 45 ÷ 5 =	**7.** 90 ÷ 9 =

Fill in the missing numbers to complete these division sums.

1. 15 ÷ ☐ = 3	**1.** 24 ÷ ☐ = 12	**1.** 80 ÷ ☐ = 10
2. 10 ÷ ☐ = 5	**2.** 30 ÷ ☐ = 6	**2.** 26 ÷ ☐ = 13
3. 18 ÷ ☐ = 9	**3.** ☐ ÷ 10 = 8	**3.** 45 ÷ ☐ = 9
4. 12 ÷ ☐ = 3	**4.** 35 ÷ ☐ = 7	**4.** 32 ÷ ☐ = 8
5. 9 ÷ ☐ = 3	**5.** 70 ÷ ☐ = 7	**5.** 21 ÷ ☐ = 7
6. 8 ÷ ☐ = 4	**6.** 24 ÷ ☐ = 6	**6.** 240 ÷ ☐ = 24
7. 24 ÷ ☐ = 6	**7.** ☐ ÷ 5 = 9	**7.** 50 ÷ ☐ = 25

Training Tips

 Dividing by two is the same as halving.

 Remember your times tables. These will help you with division.

Doubles and halves

Doubling means adding two of the same number together or multiplying by 2.

Double 8 = 8 + 8 = 8 × 2 = 16

Double all of these numbers.

Bronze

1. 8	**2.** 20
3. 12	**4.** 14
5. 50	**6.** 25
7. 11	**8.** 6
9. 35	**10.** 15

Silver

1. 15	**2.** 25
3. 50	**4.** 19
5. 17	**6.** 35
7. 100	**8.** 45
9. 150	**10.** 60

Gold

1. 35	**2.** 42
3. 120	**4.** 800
5. 29	**6.** 350
7. 1400	**8.** 48
9. 33	**10.** 3600

Halving is the same as dividing by two.

Half of 24 = 24 ÷ 2 = 12

Halve all of these numbers.

1. 18	**2.** 20
3. 60	**4.** 10
5. 14	**6.** 100
7. 80	**8.** 16
9. 90	**10.** 70

1. 40	**2.** 36
3. 200	**4.** 150
5. 180	**6.** 500
7. 32	**8.** 70
9. 38	**10.** 600

1. 900	**2.** 84
3. 96	**4.** 1400
5. 2600	**6.** 72
7. 860	**8.** 3800
9. 64	**10.** 920

 **Training Tips**

 When you double a whole number the answer is always even.

Halving an even number always gives you a whole number.

Division facts

See how quickly you can answer these division facts.

Bronze

1. 10 ÷ 2 =
2. 15 ÷ 5 =
3. 8 ÷ 2 =
4. 60 ÷ 10 =
5. 12 ÷ 2 =
6. 20 ÷ 10 =
7. 20 ÷ 5 =
8. 90 ÷ 10 =
9. 35 ÷ 5 =
10. 18 ÷ 2 =

Silver

1. 12 ÷ 4 =
2. 35 ÷ 5 =
3. 90 ÷ 10 =
4. 18 ÷ 2 =
5. 15 ÷ 3 =
6. 110 ÷ 10 =
7. 12 ÷ 2 =
8. 8 ÷ 4 =
9. 9 ÷ 3 =
10. 10 ÷ 10 =

Gold

1. 45 ÷ 5 =
2. 180 ÷ 10 =
3. 15 ÷ 3 =
4. 36 ÷ 4 =
5. 18 ÷ 9 =
6. 22 ÷ 2 =
7. 150 ÷ 10 =
8. 10 ÷ 10 =
9. 5 ÷ 1 =
10. 21 ÷ 3 =

Use the facts you know to work out the missing numbers.

1. 10 ÷ ☐ = 5
2. 40 ÷ ☐ = 4
3. 30 ÷ ☐ = 6
4. 18 ÷ ☐ = 9
5. 25 ÷ ☐ = 5

1. 12 ÷ ☐ = 4
2. 45 ÷ ☐ = 9
3. 100 ÷ ☐ = 10
4. 18 ÷ ☐ = 9
5. 21 ÷ ☐ = 7

1. 36 ÷ ☐ = 9
2. 35 ÷ ☐ = 7
3. 10 ÷ ☐ = 1
4. 21 ÷ ☐ = 7
5. 22 ÷ ☐ = 11

Training Tips

Use your times tables to help you work out division sums.
4 × 5 = 20 so 20 ÷ 5 = 4

Division with remainders

Sometimes numbers do not divide exactly and there are remainders.

16 ÷ 3 is 5 remainder 1

Work out these division sums and show the remainders.

Bronze

1. 10 ÷ 3 =

2. 14 ÷ 4 =

3. 8 ÷ 3 =

4. 17 ÷ 5 =

5. 9 ÷ 2 =

6. 32 ÷ 10 =

7. 20 ÷ 3 =

8. 18 ÷ 5 =

9. 17 ÷ 4 =

10. 10 ÷ 4 =

Silver

1. 22 ÷ 4 =

2. 45 ÷ 10 =

3. 23 ÷ 2 =

4. 68 ÷ 10 =

5. 17 ÷ 3 =

6. 24 ÷ 5 =

7. 31 ÷ 4 =

8. 33 ÷ 5 =

9. 54 ÷ 10 =

10. 19 ÷ 2 =

Gold

1. 34 ÷ 4 =

2. 146 ÷ 10 =

3. 35 ÷ 2 =

4. 49 ÷ 5 =

5. 29 ÷ 3 =

6. 41 ÷ 2 =

7. 78 ÷ 10 =

8. 25 ÷ 4 =

9. 103 ÷ 10 =

10. 28 ÷ 5 =

Training Tips

The remainder must be smaller than the number you are dividing by. Check your answers!

Rounding up or down

Sometimes when dividing numbers to solve a problem there is a remainder.

You may need to decide whether to round the answer up or down depending on what the problem is asking.

Let's have a look...

Tickets cost £5 each and Tom has £37 to spend. How many can he buy?

$37 \div 5 = 7$ remainder 2

This answer must be rounded down to 7, as Tom does not have enough money for 8 tickets.

Sita has 23 cakes. Each box holds 4 cakes. How many boxes does she need?

$23 \div 4 = 5$ remainder 3

This answer must be rounded up to 6 to make sure all the cakes are in a box.

Now try these:

Bronze

1. Tickets cost £2 each. Beth has £11. How many can she buy?

2. Tony has 17 cakes. Each box holds 4. How many boxes does he need?

3. There are 16 cakes and 5 children. How many can they each have?

4. How many strips of 10 cm ribbon can be cut from 63 cm?

5. There are 23 children. A table seats 5. How many tables are needed?

6. Juice cartons are sold in packs of 4. Sophie needs 30. How many packs must she buy?

7. There can be no more than 3 flowers in each vase. Sonny has 17 flowers. How many vases will he need?

8. At the end of a party 37 balloons are shared between 10 children. How many do they each get?

9. There are 26 children. How many teams of 5 can be made?

10. Amy needs 85p to buy a comic. She saves 10p a week. How many weeks will it take her to buy her comic?

Training Tips

Make sure your answer is sensible and you have rounded the right way.

Multiplication is the opposite operation. Use it to check your answers.

Rounding up or down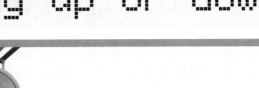

Silver

1. Tickets cost £3 each. Beth has £19. How many can she buy?

2. Tony has 23 cakes. Each box holds 4. How many boxes does he need?

3. There are 28 cakes and 5 children. How many can they each have?

4. How many strips of 10 cm ribbon can be cut from 163 cm?

5. There are 43 children. A table seats 5. How many tables are needed?

6. Juice cartons are sold in packs of 4. Sophie needs 41. How many packs must she buy?

7. There can be no more than 3 flowers in each vase. Sonny has 32 flowers. How many vases will he need?

8. At the end of a party 87 balloons are shared between 10 children. How many do they each get?

9. There are 33 children. How many teams of 5 can be made? How many children are not able to join in?

10. Amy needs £1.25 to buy a comic. She saves 10p a week. How many weeks will it take her to buy her comic?

Gold

1. Tickets cost £6 each. Beth has £23.50. How many can she buy?

2. Tony has 42 cakes. Each box holds 4. How many boxes does he need?

3. There are 38 cakes and 5 children. How many can they each have?

4. How many strips of 20 cm ribbon can be cut from 163 cm?

5. There are 73 children. A table seats 5. How many tables are needed?

6. Juice cartons are sold in packs of 4. Sophie needs 79. How many packs must she buy?

7. There can be no more than 3 flowers in each vase. Sonny has 61 flowers. How many vases will he need?

8. At the end of a party 187 balloons are shared between 10 children. How many do they each get?

9. There are 68 children. How many teams of 5 can be made? How many children are not able to join in?

10. Amy needs £2.20 to buy a comic. She saves 25p a week. How many weeks will it take her to buy her comic?

Multiplying and dividing by 10

A quick and easy way to multiply by 10 is to move each digit one place to the left and put zero into the units column.

T	U		H	T	U
7	6	× 10 becomes	7	6	0

Bronze

Multiply by 10:

1. 7
2. 9
3. 26
4. 10
5. 14

Silver

Multiply by 10:

1. 79
2. 90
3. 348
4. 601
5. 754

Gold

Multiply:

1. 54 × 10 =
2. 90 × 10 =
3. 147 × 100 =
4. 658 × 10 =
5. 320 × 10 =

The same rule applies for dividing but you need to move each digit one place to the right and take off the zero.

H	T	U		T	U
5	4	0	÷ 10 becomes	5	4

Divide by 10:

1. 80
2. 60
3. 170
4. 240
5. 200

Divide by 10:

1. 860
2. 450
3. 5000
4. 3040
5. 4580

Divide:

1. 850 ÷ 10 =
2. 6500 ÷ 100 =
3. 7400 ÷ 10 =
4. 9700 ÷ 100 =
5. 1000 ÷ 100 =

Training Tips

A whole number multiplied by 10 always ends in zero.

Finding quarters

Finding quarter of a number is the same as dividing by 4.
It is also the same as working out half of one half.

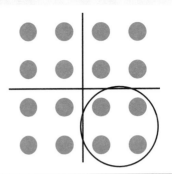

For example, to find one quarter of 16:

Half of 16 = 8

Half of 8 = 4 so one quarter of 16 is 4

Use halving to work out one quarter of each of these numbers.

Bronze	Silver	Gold
1. 8	1. 100	1. 800
2. 28	2. 140	2. 144
3. 12	3. 48	3. 1000
4. 20	4. 300	4. 500
5. 24	5. 36	5. 188
6. 40	6. 88	6. 104
7. 100	7. 60	7. 96
8. 36	8. 600	8. 300
9. 32	9. 200	9. 2000
10. 4	10. 400	10. 4400

How long is one side of a square if the total perimeter is:

1. 40 cm?	1. 200 m?	1. 1 km?
2. 16 m?	2. 48 cm?	2. 360 m?
3. 100 cm?	3. 1 m?	3. 180 cm?
4. 24 m?	4. 40 m?	4. 1 m?
5. 8 km?	5. 600 m?	5. 92 m?

 Training Tips

 Learn your 4 times table as it will help you to work out quarters!

Putting it into practice

Some of the scores have fallen off the judge's scoreboard.

Japan	10	Norway	
England	90	France	35
Spain		America	
Turkey		Denmark	8
Russia		Iceland	
Australia		Scotland	
Ireland	60	Switzerland	600
Greece		Finland	21
China		Egypt	
Morocco		Germany	
Holland		Canada	2000
Hong Kong		Austria	95
Wales		Poland	
South Africa		Mexico	
Sweden		Brazil	

Training Tips

Write down each new fact as you get it.

Putting it into practice

See if you can solve the clues below to fill in the missing scores.

Bronze

1. Norway scored 8 times as much as Japan.

2. Divide England's score by 10 to find Turkey's score.

3. Iceland scored double France's score.

4. Russia scored half of England's score.

5. Spain scored 4 times Denmark's score.

6. America scored ten times France's score.

7. Egypt scored a quarter of Ireland's score.

8. Hong Kong scored 4 × 5.

9. Divide Finland's score by 3 to find Morocco's score.

10. China scored 630 ÷ 10.

Silver

1. Australia scored 100 times as much as Denmark.

2. Scotland scored one tenth of Switzerland.

3. Iceland scored double France's score.

4. Russia scored half of England's score.

5. Greece scored 4 times as much as Ireland.

6. China scored 3 times as much as Finland.

7. Egypt scored a quarter of Ireland's score.

8. Morocco scored one fifth of 35.

9. Norway scored five multiplied by 16.

10. Mexico scored double Iceland's score.

Gold

1. Holland scored ten times as much as Finland.

2. Divide Canada's score by 100 to find Hong Kong's score.

3. Wales scored double Austria's score.

4. Poland scored half of Holland's score.

5. South Africa scored 6 times as much as Finland.

6. Mexico scored 4 times as much as France.

7. Germany scored a quarter of Switzerland's score.

8. China scored 9 × 7.

9. Sweden scored 12 × 6.

10. Brazil scored 43 × 3.

Word problems

Question: There are 100 books on a shelf. 45 of them are fiction, 25 are information books and the rest are poetry books. How many are poetry books?

1. The first thing to do is to think about what the problem is telling you. Which operations do we need to use? Add the numbers? Subtract? Multiply or divide? Or do we need to use more than one operation?

2. This problem needs addition and subtraction. Let's look.

3. We know there are 100 books altogether so...

fiction + information + poetry = 100
fiction + information = 45 + 25 = 70
The rest are poetry. 100 − 70 = 30

Answer: There must be 30 poetry books.

Look at the problems and decide which operation to use.
Work out the answers and show your sum.

Bronze

1. Two children have 12 pencils each. How many do they have altogether?

2. In her pocket Lisa has two 10p coins, three pennies and one 5p coin. How much money does she have?

3. There are 28 biscuits on a plate. If two children share them equally how many will they each have?

4. Crayons are sold in packs of 5. If Amit has 6 packs, how many crayons does he have?

5. There are 34 sweets in a packet. Joel eats 13. How many are left?

6. Mrs Brown needs 30 balloons for her party. There are 4 in a packet. How many packets will she need?

7. Siva has saved 70p of his pocket money. He wants to buy a comic that costs £1.20. How much more does he need to save?

8. 22 people are on a bus. At the next stop 5 get off and 8 get on. How many people are on the bus now?

Training Tips

Read each problem very carefully and think about what it says. It might help to draw a picture or talk about it with a friend.

Word problems

Silver

1. In a box of fruit there are 15 bananas, 12 apples and 23 pears. How many pieces of fruit are there altogether?

2. In her pocket Sari has three pound coins, one 50p, four 2p coins and a penny. How much money does she have?

3. There are 45 biscuits in the packet. How many people can have 5 each?

4. A box holds 35 nuts. How many are there in 3 boxes?

5. There are 60 coloured pencils in the box. 26 are red, 23 are blue and the rest are green. How many green pencils are there?

6. I think of a number and double it and add 5. The answer is 45. What was my number?

7. In the garden Sophie saw 3 spiders, 7 birds and 5 cats. How many legs did she see on the animals?

8. There are 31 people on the bus. 16 get on and 20 get off. How many people are now on the bus?

Gold

1. There are 45 apples in a box. 28 children have one each. How many are left?

2. There are 24 pears in a box. How many people can have 4 each?

3. Franco has a five pound note, three 50 pence coins, four 5 pence coins and three pennies. How much money does he have altogether?

4. There are 78 books on the top shelf and 42 on the bottom shelf. I take 29 of them away. How many are left?

5. A beetle has 6 legs. How many legs do 9 beetles have?

6. Tom has 27 cars. Jamie has twice as many. How many do they have altogether?

7. In the garden Sophie saw 10 spiders, 15 birds and 5 cats. How many legs did she see on the animals?

8. There are 36 children in the class. Half of them have packed lunch. 10 children have school dinners and the rest go home. How many children go home for lunch?

Training Tips

Check your answers by doing the problem again or doing the opposite operation.

Number puzzles

What numbers can you make using the numbers 4, 10 and 5 and the × + and = signs?

$4 × 10 = 40$ $4 × 5 = 20$ $5 × 10 = 50$ $5 + 4 = 9$

$4 + 10 = 14$ $5 + 10 = 15$ $4 + 5 + 10 = 19$

Now it's your turn!

Bronze

1. Use the digits 1 and 2 and the signs + − and = as many times as you like to make all the numbers from 0 to 10.

2. What do you notice when you add two odd numbers?

3. Fill in the missing signs:
   $16 * 2 = 8$
   $21 * 14 = 35$
   $4 * 5 = 20$
   $30 * 17 = 13$

4. Find five different ways to add odd numbers to make 15.

Silver

1. Use the digits 1 and 2 and the signs + − and = as many times as you like to make all the numbers from 0 to 10.

2. What do you notice when you add three odd numbers?

3. Fill in the missing signs:
   $73 * 88 = 161$
   $160 * 41 = 119$
   $7 * 8 = 56$
   $95 * 5 = 19$

4. Find five different ways to add odd numbers to make 45.

Gold

1. Find three consecutive numbers that add up to 24.

2. Fill in the missing signs and numbers:
   $120 * ? = 12$
   $30 * ? = 46$
   $45 * ? = 9$
   $50 * ? = 24$

3. Find a pair of numbers with a difference of 11 and a total of 35.

4. Find five different ways to add odd numbers to make 75.

Number puzzles

Bronze

Silver

Gold

5. Find three pairs of numbers with a difference of 5 and a total greater than 20.

6. Use 1, 4 and 5 and + − and = . How many different numbers can you make?

7. Find a pair of numbers with a total of 20 and a difference that is greater than 5.

8. Use three dice. How many different ways are there to score 12?

9. Find 3 two-digit numbers where the sum of the digits is odd.

---

5. Find a pair of numbers with a difference of 5 and a total less than 20.

6. Make a triangle shape using the numbers 1 to 6 so that the sum of each side of the triangle is 12.

7. Use three dice. What even totals can you get?

8. Find 5 ways of adding odd numbers to make 30.

9. Find 3 three-digit numbers where the sum of the digits is 10.

---

5. Draw three circles. Use each of the numbers 1 to 9. Write them in the circles so that each circle has a total of 15.

6. Using the digits 2 and 3 as many times as you like and all the signs, make the numbers from 0 to 10.

7. Make a triangle shape using the numbers 1 to 6 so that the sum of each side of the triangle is the same.

8. Find 3 four-digit numbers where the sum of the digits is 10.

9. Find a pair of numbers with a difference of 5 and a total between 15 and 20.

Training Tips

The way to solve some of these problems is by guessing first. Look at your answers and see what needs to be changed to get the correct answer. Keep trying!

Money – finding ways to pay

Look at each of these sets of coins and work out how much there is altogether.

 Bronze

1. 20p + 20p + 10p + 2p + 2p + 1 p = ☐

2. 50p + 20p + 10p + 5p + 5p + 1p + 1p + 1p = ☐

3. 50p + 50p + 10p + 2p + 2p + 2p = ☐

4. £1 + 50p + 10p + 2p + 1p + 1p + 1p = ☐

5. £1 + £1 + 50p + 10p + 10p + 5p = ☐

6. 20p + 50p + £1 + 20p + £1 + 1p = ☐

7. 10p + 50p + 10p + £1 + £1 + 5p + 5p + 5p = ☐

 **Silver**

1. £1 + 50p + 20p + 10p + 10p + 5p + 5p + 2p + 2p = ☐

2. £2 + £2 + 20p + 10p + 5p + 2p + 1p + 1p = ☐

3. £5 + £1 + 50p + 10p + 20p + 5p + 5p = ☐

4. £5 + £10 + 50p + 50p + 20p + 10p + 10p = ☐

5. £20 + £10 + £2 + 20p + 50p + 10p + 1p = ☐

6. £20 + 20p + 10p + 50p + 10p + 2p + 2p + 1p + 1p = ☐

7. £2 + £1 + £2 + 50p + 10p + 2p + 5p + 1p + 1p = ☐

 Gold

1. £10 + £5 + 50p + 10p + 2p + 2p + 1p + 1p = ☐

2. £2 + £1 + £5 + 50p + 10p + 5p + 1p + 2p + 1p = ☐

3. 4 × £2 + 50p + 10p + 10p + 5p + 5p + 1p + 1p = ☐

4. 3 × £5 + 20p + 10p + £1 + 50p + 1p + 1p + 2p + £1 = ☐

5. £10 + £10 + £20 + 50p + 10p + 50p + 2p + 2p + 5p = ☐

6. £5 + 1p + 1p + 5p + 5p + 2p + 10p + 50p + £2 + £1 = ☐

7. 5p + 10p + 50p + 1p + 1p + 2p + £1 + £5 + 50p + 1p = ☐

 **Training Tips**

 Remember £1 = 100 pence

 When adding up coins start with the biggest number first.

Money – finding ways to pay

Bronze

8. £2 + 20p + 10p + 2p + 2p + 1p + 1p + 10p = ☐

9. 10p + 1p + 10p + 2p + 5p + £1 + 20p = ☐

10. 50p + 50p + 50p + 20p + 10p + £2 = ☐

Silver

8. 20p + 10p + 50p + 2p + 10p + £1 + £2 + 50p = ☐

9. 10p + 50p + £5 + 2p + 2p + 1p + 10p + £1 = ☐

10. 20p + £5 + 50p + £1 + £2 + 2p + 1p + 5p + 5p = ☐

Gold

8. £10 + £5 + 10p + 50p + 1p + 20p + 2p + 5p + 5p + £1 = ☐

9. 20p + 50p + £1 + £2 + £1 + £5 + £10 + 50p + 1p + 1p + 2p = ☐

10. 5 × £2 + 20p + 10p + 50p + 50p + 10p + 2p + 1p + 1p + 1p = ☐

Use coins and notes to find three different ways to make these amounts.

Example

75p = 50p, 20p, 5p   or 20p, 20p, 20p, 10p, 5p   or 50p, 10p, 10p, 5p

1. 50p	**1.** £2.50	**1.** £4.46
2. £1	**2.** £1.38	**2.** £5.03
3. 65p	**3.** £1.04	**3.** £2.98
4. 48p	**4.** 99p	**4.** £3.50
5. 73p	**5.** £1.27	**5.** £4.25

Training Tips

Look for pairs you know, such as 50p + 50p = £1

Explaining your methods

Sometimes it is not the answer that is important but how you got there.
It is good to show what you did to get an answer even if you did it in your head.

Example 1

Ashley worked out that 12 + 15 = 27. How could he have got the answer?

One way could be to add 12 and 10 to get 22. Then add on 5 to get 27.

Another way could be to show it on a number line.

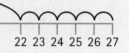

Example 2

Tina worked out that 4 × 5 = 20. How did she get the answer?

One way could be to use repeated addition 5 + 5 + 5 + 5 = 20
Pictures also help.

**For these sums the answers have already been worked out.
Show how they could have been done.**

 Bronze

1. 8 + 6 = 14
2. 30 – 12 = 18
3. 16 ÷ 4 = 4
4. 7 × 2 = 14
5. 16 + 17 = 33
6. 23 + 35 = 58
7. 45 – 21 = 24
8. 20 ÷ 5 = 4
9. 26 ÷ 2 = 13
10. 6 × 3 = 18

 **Silver**

1. 26 + 32 = 58
2. 75 – 34 = 41
3. 12 × 3 = 36
4. 48 ÷ 2 = 24
5. 48 – 37 = 11
6. 24 + 66 = 90
7. 10 × 5 = 50
8. 24 ÷ 4 = 6
9. 25 × 2 = 50
10. 60 – 39 = 21

Gold

1. 124 + 68 = 192
2. 147 – 35 = 112
3. 56 ÷ 2 = 28
4. 42 × 2 = 84
5. 56 + 21 + 14 = 91
6. 296 – 153 = 143
7. 36 ÷ 4 = 9
8. 14 × 10 = 140
9. 23 + 34 + 71 = 128
10. 158 – 39 = 119

 **Training Tips**

 Number lines are a good way to work out addition and subtraction sums.

 Partitioning two-digit numbers into tens and units helps with addition.

Finding totals

Sports Café

SALAD £2.20	**PIZZA** £1.60	**FISH** £3.50	**CHICKEN** £2.80
PASTA £6.50	**CURRY** £7.20	**SANDWICH** £1.05	**HOT DOG** £1.25
COFFEE 75p	**TEA** 80p	**COLA** 50p	**LEMONADE** 40p

How much would the following cost?

 Bronze

1. A sandwich and a cola

2. Hot dog and a salad

3. Fish and a salad

4. Salad and a coffee

5. Two sandwiches

 Silver

1. Pasta and fish

2. Chicken and a salad

3. Pasta and a coffee

4. Curry and a cola

5. Two pizzas

 Gold

1. Pasta and chicken

2. Two curries

3. Pizza, salad and a coffee

4. A sandwich, a hot dog and a pizza

5. Three chickens

What can you buy for:

1. £4?	*1.* £8?	*1.* £10?
2. £3?	*2.* £7?	*2.* £8?
3. £2?	*3.* £10?	*3.* £15?
4. £5?	*4.* £7.50?	*4.* £20?
5. £6?	*5.* £3?	*5.* £10.50?

 *Training Tips*

 When working out totals add up the pounds first then the pence.

Money problems

Sports Shop		
T-SHIRTS £4.50	**SWEATSHIRTS** £8	**CAP** £5.25
TRACKSUIT £10.75	**FOOTBALL** £3	**BAT** £7.50
GLOVES £6	**BADGE** £1	**SOCKS** £2

Jo saves 20p a week. How long will it take for her to be able to afford a pair of socks?

Jo saves 20p in one week, so in two weeks she will have 40p. In three weeks she will have 60p. She needs 200p.

So, ☐ × 20 + 200. It must be 10.
It will take Jo 10 weeks to save enough for the socks.

Try these.

1. Amrit saves 50p a week. How many weeks must he save to buy a football?

2. Sam saves £1 a month. How long must he save to afford a cap?

3. Priya saves 20p a week. How long will it take her to afford a badge?

4. Saul buys a T-shirt. How much change will he get from £10?

5. Luke buys a bat. He gives the shopkeeper a £10 note. What coins will he get in his change?

6. Rebecca buys two pairs of gloves. How much change will she get from £20?

7. Ella buys two sweatshirts. She pays with two notes and one coin. What were they?

8. Pete has £10 to spend. What two items could he buy?

9. How many footballs can be bought for £20?

10. Jordan buys a T-shirt. He uses three coins to pay for it. What could they be?

Training Tips

If the answer is money don't forget to write the £ or the p sign.

Money problems

1. Amrit saves 50p a week. How many weeks must he save to buy a cap?

2. Sam saves £1 a month. How long must he save to afford a tracksuit?

3. Priya saves 20p a week. How long will it take her to afford a T-shirt?

4. Saul buys a tracksuit. How much change will he get from £20?

5. Luke buys a cap. He gives the shopkeeper a £10 note. What coins will he get in his change?

6. Rebecca buys two bats. How much change will she get from £20?

7. Ella buys two T-shirts. She pays with one note and eight coins. What were they?

8. Pete has £20 to spend. What two items could he buy?

9. How many tracksuits can be bought for £50?

10. Jordan buys a bat. He uses five coins to pay for it. What could they be?

1. Amrit saves 50p a week. How many weeks must he save to buy a sweatshirt and gloves?

2. Sam saves £1 a month. How long must he save to afford a tracksuit and a T-shirt?

3. Priya saves 20p a week. How long will it take her to afford a cap?

4. Saul buys a tracksuit. How much change will he get from £20?

5. Luke buys a cap. He gives the shopkeeper a £10 note. What coins will he get in his change?

6. Rebecca buys three tracksuits. How much change will she get from £50?

7. Ella buys two caps. She pays with two notes and five coins. What were they?

8. Pete spends exactly £16. What two items did he buy?

9. How many footballs can be bought for £50?

10. Jordan buys a cap. He uses 6 coins to pay for it. What could they be?

Calculating change

Drawing number lines is a good way to calculate change.

Example

Sanjiv bought cola that cost 75p. He gave the waitress £2.
How much was his change?

His change was

5p + 10p + 10p + £1 = £1.25

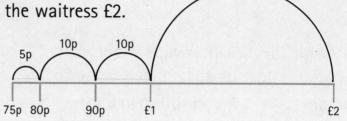

Sports Café

SALAD £2.20	**PIZZA** £1.60	**FISH** £3.50	**CHICKEN** £2.80
PASTA £6.50	**CURRY** £7.20	**SANDWICH** £1.05	**HOT DOG** £1.25
COFFEE 75p	**TEA** 80p	**COLA** 50p	**LEMONADE** 40p

Calculate the change when the following items are bought
with the amount shown.

Bronze

1. Tea	£1
2. Pizza	£2
3. Lemonade	£1
4. Chicken	£3
5. Salad	£3
6. Hot dog	£2
7. Cola	£2
8. Fish	£5
9. Pasta	£7
10. Sandwich	£2

Silver

1. Sandwich	£2
2. Curry	£10
3. Fish	£5
4. Chicken	£5
5. Hot dog	£1.50
6. Salad	£5
7. Pizza	£5
8. Coffee	£2
9. Pasta	£10
10. Lemonade	£2

Gold

1. Sandwich	£5
2. Hot dog	£5
3. Pizza	£10
4. Curry	£10
5. Chicken	£10
6. Two pizzas	£10
7. Hot dog and tea	£10
8. Two curries	£20
9. Pasta and coffee	£10
10. Fish and salad	£20

Training Tips

Count up to the nearest pound to calculate the pence and then count up the pounds.

Measuring length

Short lengths can be measured in cm or mm. 1 cm is the same as 10 mm.

Warm up

a) Measure these lines to the nearest cm or half cm.

1. _____

2. _____

3. _____

4. _____

5. _____

b) Measure these lines and give the answer as mm.

1. _____

2. _____

3. _____

4. _____

5. _____

Let's practise drawing some lines.
Remember to use a ruler and to start at zero. Make sure they are all straight!

 Bronze

Draw lines that are these lengths:

1. 8 cm
2. 12 cm
3. $6\frac{1}{2}$ cm
4. 9 cm
5. $5\frac{1}{2}$ cm
6. $3\frac{1}{2}$ cm
7. 14 cm
8. $2\frac{1}{2}$ cm
9. 7 cm
10. 10 cm

 Silver

Draw lines that are these lengths:

1. 15 cm
2. $12\frac{1}{2}$ cm
3. $9\frac{1}{2}$ cm
4. $\frac{1}{2}$ cm
5. 70 mm
6. 45 mm
7. 16 cm
8. 85 mm
9. $3\frac{1}{2}$ cm
10. 25 mm

Gold

Use some squared paper. Draw rectangles that have sides these lengths:

1. 5 cm and 8 cm
2. 70 mm and 30 mm
3. 2 cm and 90 mm
4. $4\frac{1}{2}$ cm and 6 cm
5. 75 mm and 45 mm
6. 60 mm and $3\frac{1}{2}$ cm
7. 100 mm and 10 cm
8. $5\frac{1}{2}$ cm and $8\frac{1}{2}$ cm
9. 120 mm and 30 mm
10. 14 cm and 2 cm

 **Training Tips**

 When using a ruler, make sure the line starts at zero.

• 10 mm = 1 cm
• 5 mm = $\frac{1}{2}$ cm

Length problems

Length is measured in millimetres (mm), centimetres (cm), metres (m) or kilometres (km).

| 1 cm = 10 mm | 1 m = 100 cm | 1 km = 1000 m |

Fill in the missing numbers to make these correct:

 Bronze

1. 3 cm = ☐ mm
2. 5 m = ☐ cm
3. 1 m 50 cm = ☐ cm
4. 4 km = ☐ m

 Silver

1. 8 cm = ☐ mm
2. 12 m = ☐ cm
3. 2.5 m = ☐ cm
4. 5 km = ☐ m

 Gold

1. 1 m = ☐ mm
2. 3.05 m = ☐ cm
3. 150 cm = ☐ m
4. 8 km = ☐ m

Let's solve some problems!

1. My cat is 25 cm tall. My dog is 15 cm taller. How tall is my dog?

2. I am 1 m 5 cm tall. My dad is twice as tall. How tall is he?

3. How many 10 cm pieces of ribbon can I cut from 1 m?

---

1. It is 7 km from Tom's house to Jane's. Fred lives another 5 km away. How far is it to Fred's house? How many m?

2. How many 10 cm pieces of ribbon can I cut from $2\frac{1}{2}$ m?

3. Two pieces of string are 55 cm and 31 cm long. What is the difference in their lengths?

---

1. Two shelves are 65 cm and 86 cm long. What is their total length in cm?

2. I am digging a tunnel that is 5 m long. I have dug 2 m 25 cm so far. How much further do I have to go?

3. A garden is rectangular. The short sides measure 8 m. The long sides are twice as long. How much fence will I need to go all the way round?

 **Training Tips**

10 mm = 1 cm
100 cm = 1 m
1000 m = 1 km

Mass problems

The mass or weight of an object is measured in grams (g) or kilograms (kg).

$$1\,kg = 1000\,g$$

Fill in the missing numbers to make these correct:

 Bronze

1. 3 kg = ☐ g
2. 6000 g = ☐ kg
3. 1000 g = ☐ kg
4. 8 kg = ☐ g

 Silver

1. 7 kg = ☐ g
2. 4500 g = ☐ kg
3. $2\frac{1}{2}$ kg = ☐ g
4. 9000 g = ☐ kg

 Gold

1. 10 kg = ☐ g
2. 3500 g = ☐ kg
3. $7\frac{1}{4}$ kg = ☐ g
4. 5250 g = ☐ kg

Let's solve some mass problems.

1. A box contains 5 kg of potatoes. How many boxes are needed for 20 kg?

2. A bag of sugar weighs 200 g. How much would 4 bags weigh?

3. Mark weighed 4 kg when he was born. He is now twice as heavy. How much does he weigh?

4. Sally bought 100 g of sweets. She ate half of them. How much does she have left?

---

1. Sally bought 100 g of sweets. She ate a quarter of them. How much does she have left?

2. Joe weighs 17 kg. His dad weighs twice as much. How much do they weigh together?

3. An apple weighs about 50 g. How many apples will you get in 1 kg?

4. A bag of flour weighs 250 g. How much would 6 bags weigh?

---

1. A potato weighs about 250 g. How much would 10 potatoes weigh?

2. Joe weighs 26 kg. His dad weighs twice as much. How much do they weigh together?

3. Sally bought 1 kg of bananas. She ate a quarter of them and gave 300 g to her friend. How much does she have left?

4. An apple weighs about 50 g. How many apples will you get in $1\frac{1}{2}$ kg?

 **Training Tips**

 1000 g = 1 kg   250 g = $\frac{1}{4}$ kg
500 g = $\frac{1}{2}$ kg   750 g = $\frac{3}{4}$ kg

Measuring mass

The mass of an object tells us how much it weighs.
Light objects can be measured in grams (g).
Heavy objects are measured using kilograms (kg).

| 1 kilogram = 1000 grams |

Write these weights in kg or g.

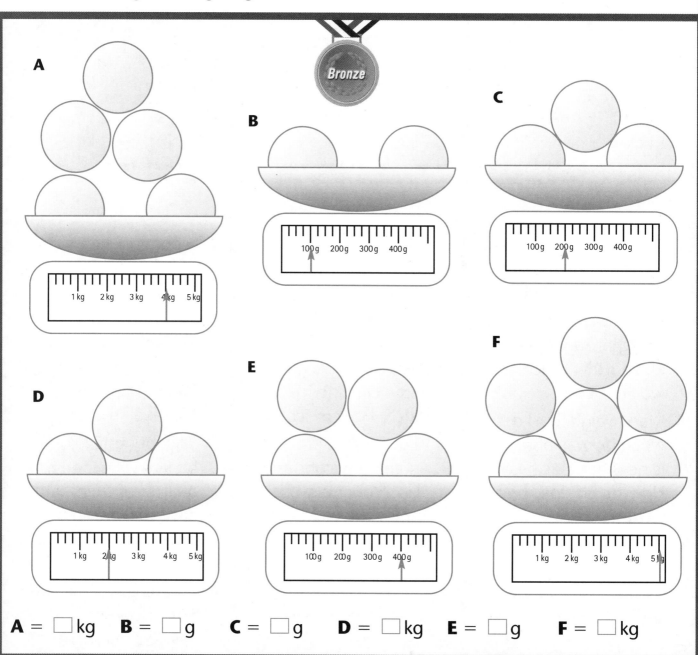

A = ☐ kg **B** = ☐ g **C** = ☐ g **D** = ☐ kg **E** = ☐ g **F** = ☐ kg

 **Training Tips**

 Reading scales is like reading a clock. The numbers and the pointer go the same way round. If the pointer is between two numbers look to see which one it has gone past.

Measuring mass

Write these weights in kg or g.

Silver

A

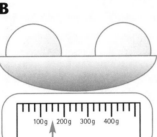
B

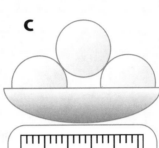
C

D

1 kg 2 kg 3 kg 4 kg 5 kg

100 g 200 g 300 g 400 g

100 g 200 g 300 g 400 g

1 kg 2 kg 3 kg 4 kg 5 kg

A = ☐ kg **B** = ☐ g **C** = ☐ g **D** = ☐ kg

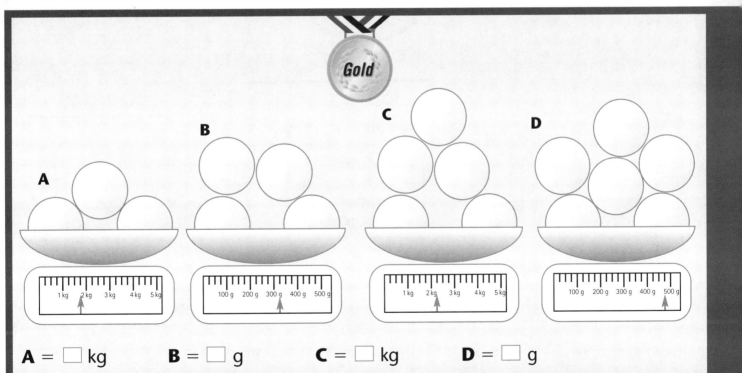
Gold

A B C D

1 kg 2 kg 3 kg 4 kg 5 kg

100 g 200 g 300 g 400 g 500 g

1 kg 2 kg 3 kg 4 kg 5 kg

100 g 200 g 300 g 400 g 500 g

A = ☐ kg **B** = ☐ g **C** = ☐ kg **D** = ☐ g

Measuring capacity

Capacity is measured in litres (l) and millilitres (ml).

There are 1000 ml in one litre.

Write these capacities in l or ml.

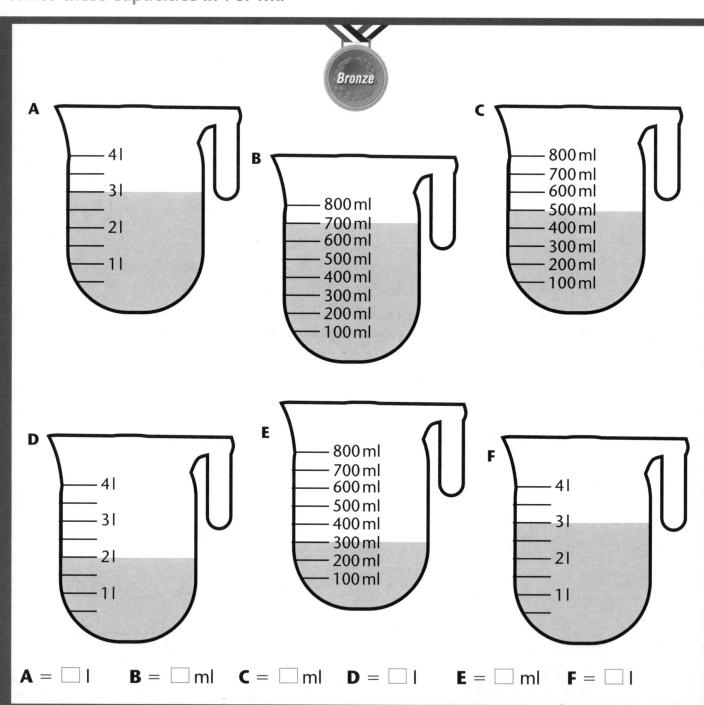

A = ☐ l   **B** = ☐ ml   **C** = ☐ ml   **D** = ☐ l   **E** = ☐ ml   **F** = ☐ l

Training Tips

 Look closely at the scale and decide if it is in ml or l.

 1000 ml = 1 l
500 ml = ½ l
250 ml = ¼ l

Measuring capacity

Write these capacities in l or ml.

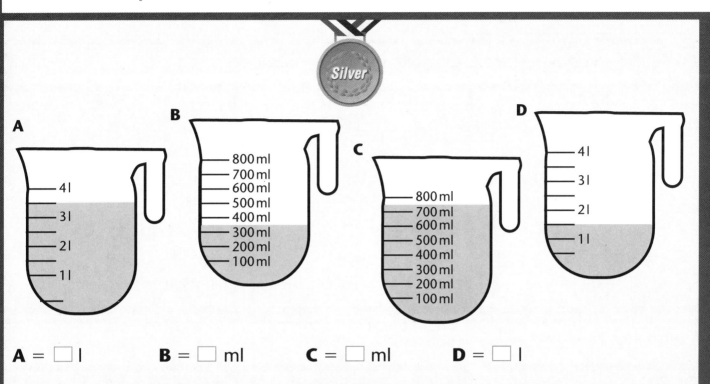

A = ☐ l   B = ☐ ml   C = ☐ ml   D = ☐ l

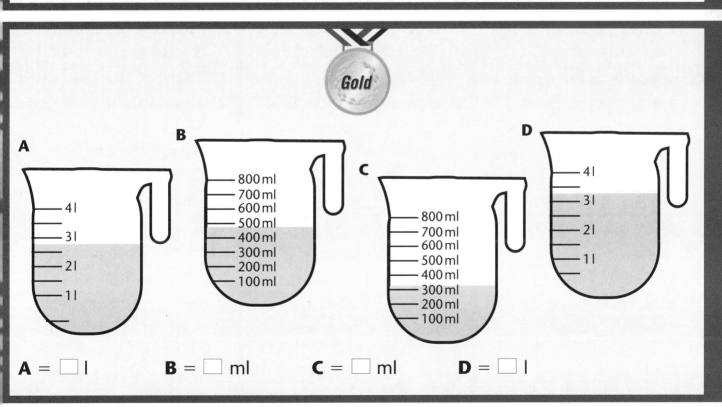

A = ☐ l   B = ☐ ml   C = ☐ ml   D = ☐ l

Training Tips

 A can of cola holds 330 ml.

 A carton of orange juice holds 1 l or 1000 ml.

Capacity problems

The capacity of a liquid is measured in litres (l) and millilitres (ml).

1 l = 1000 ml

Fill in the missing numbers to make these correct:

Bronze

1. 7 l = ☐ ml

2. 4000 ml = ☐ l

3. 6000 ml = ☐ l

4. 9 l = ☐ ml

Silver

1. 6 l = ☐ ml

2. 7500 ml = ☐ l

3. $5\frac{1}{2}$ l = ☐ ml

4. $1\frac{1}{2}$ l = ☐ ml

Gold

1. 10 l = ☐ ml

2. 7500 ml = ☐ l

3. $4\frac{1}{2}$ l = ☐ ml

4. 8250 ml = ☐ l

Let's solve some capacity problems.

Bronze

1. How many 200 ml bottles of perfume can be filled from 1 l?

2. A bottle of lemonade holds 100 ml. How much can 17 bottles hold?

3. The bottle of cola held 1 l. Ella drank 400 ml. How much was left?

4. Steven took 15 ml of medicine three times a day. How much did he take every day?

Silver

1. Steven took 15 ml of medicine three times a day. How much did he take in 2 days?

2. How many 100 ml bottles of perfume can be filled from $1\frac{1}{2}$ l?

3. The bottle of cola held 1 l. Ella drank 250 ml. How much was left?

4. Kenny had buckets holding 2 l, 1500 ml and $4\frac{1}{2}$ l. How much water did he have?

Gold

1. Steven took 15 ml of medicine three times a day. How much did he take in one week?

2. The bottle of cola held 1 l. Ella drank half and gave 150 ml to her brother. How much was left?

3. How many 50 ml bottles of perfume can be filled from $\frac{1}{4}$ l?

4. Kenny had buckets holding $1\frac{1}{2}$ l, 250 ml and $1\frac{1}{2}$ l. How much water did he have?

Training Tips

1000 ml = 1 l	250 ml = $\frac{1}{4}$ l
500 ml = $\frac{1}{2}$ l	750 ml = $\frac{3}{4}$ l

Choosing units

The units of measurement we have learned are:

ml   l   g   kg   mm   cm   m   km

For each of the measurements below decide which units have been used.

Example
The baby weighed 4☐ when she was born.
It is a measurement of mass so the units must be g or kg.
4g is a very light weight so the baby must have weighed 4kg.

Bronze

1. A toy car weighs 300☐
2. George is 96☐ tall
3. A glass held 300☐ of milk
4. The ladybird was 9☐ long
5. Lucy weighed 12☐
6. The bath held 36☐ of water
7. The table is 50☐ tall
8. The room is 12☐ long
9. The cake recipe needed 250☐ of flour
10. The playground is 1☐ long

Silver

1. Sam bought 100☐ of sweets
2. My page is 21☐ wide
3. This melon weighs more than 2☐
4. I have to take 5☐ of medicine every day
5. My toy car is 90☐ long
6. Our playground is ½☐ wide
7. I am more than 1☐ tall
8. A big bottle of cola holds 2☐
9. My cat is 30☐ tall
10. This paint can holds 500☐ of paint

Gold

1. An apple weighs about 50☐
2. My shoelaces are 30☐ long
3. I need ½☐ of potatoes for dinner
4. The playground is 1½☐ long
5. This pencil is 150☐ long
6. I can jump nearly 1☐
7. A spoon holds about 5☐
8. My dad is 1½☐ tall
9. This glass holds ½☐
10. It is 25☐ to Grandma's house

Training Tips

If something is light it will only be a few grams.

If something is very small it is probably measured in mm.

Negative numbers (temperature)

When it gets very cold the temperature drops below 0 degrees.
We then read the scale in negative numbers.
Negative numbers go back from zero.

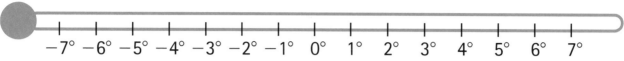

−7° −6° −5° −4° −3° −2° −1° 0° 1° 2° 3° 4° 5° 6° 7°

We write temperatures as °C.

Look at the thermometers below and write the temperature shown.

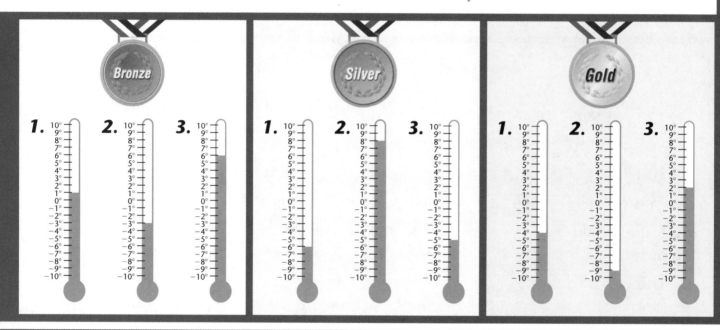

Bronze   Silver   Gold

1.   2.   3.   1.   2.   3.   1.   2.   3.

**Draw the thermometers described below and colour
in to show the temperatures.**

Draw thermometers from −10° to 0°. Show:	Draw thermometers from −5° to 5°. Show:	Draw thermometers from −10° to 10°. Mark the scale in twos. Show:
1. −9 degrees	**1.** −3 degrees	**1.** −8 degrees
2. −3 degrees	**2.** 3 degrees	**2.** 6 degrees
3. 0 degrees	**3.** 0 degrees	**3.** 7 degrees
4. −2 degrees	**4.** 4 degrees	**4.** −2 degrees
5. −8 degrees	**5.** −5 degrees	**5.** −5 degrees

Training Tips

When writing negative numbers, count backwards from zero instead of forwards.

Units of time

There are lots of units of time.
The shortest is seconds and the longest is years.

60 seconds = 1 minute   60 minutes = 1 hour   24 hours = 1 day

7 days = 1 week   12 months = 1 year   52 weeks = 1 year   365 days = 1 year

Fill in the missing numbers to complete this information.

Bronze

1. 2 weeks = ☐ days

2. One year =
☐ months

3. 60 seconds = ☐

4. 24 hours = ☐

5. 2 years = ☐ months

6. 1 year = ☐ days

7. 1 minute =
☐ seconds

8. 7 days = ☐

9. 60 minutes = ☐

10. 52 weeks = ☐

Silver

1. 2 years = ☐ months

2. 4 weeks = ☐ days

3. 2 minutes =
☐ seconds

4. 72 hours = ☐ days

5. 2 years = ☐ weeks

6. 1 year = ☐ days

7. 1 month = about
☐ days

8. 10 hours =
☐ minutes

9. 14 days = ☐

10. $\frac{1}{4}$ year = ☐ months

Gold

1. $1\frac{1}{2}$ years =
☐ months

2. 6 weeks = ☐ days

3. 5 minutes =
☐ seconds

4. 3 days = ☐ hours

5. 2 years = ☐ days

6. 6 months = about
☐ days

7. A fortnight = ☐ days

8. $\frac{1}{6}$ hour = ☐ minutes

9. 30 days = ☐

10. 3 years = ☐ weeks

Training Tips

 A fortnight is another name for two weeks!

 In a leap year there are 366 days. 2004 and 2008 are leap years.

Reading times

We use two different types of clock to tell the time –
an analogue clock and a digital clock.

These two clocks both show the same time.
It is 'forty minutes past five o'clock'.
A better way to say that is 'twenty to six'.

analogue   *digital*

Look at the clocks below and write in words the times they show.

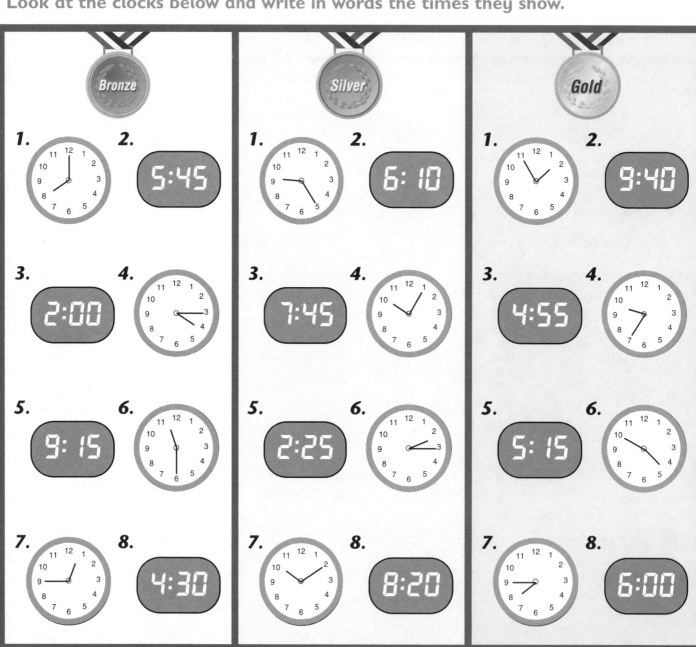

Bronze

1. [analogue clock]   2. 5:45

3. 2:00   4. [analogue clock]

5. 9:15   6. [analogue clock]

7. [analogue clock]   8. 4:30

Silver

1. [analogue clock]   2. 6:10

3. 7:45   4. [analogue clock]

5. 2:25   6. [analogue clock]

7. [analogue clock]   8. 8:20

Gold

1. [analogue clock]   2. 9:40

3. 4:55   4. [analogue clock]

5. 5:15   6. [analogue clock]

7. [analogue clock]   8. 6:00

Training Tips

When drawing the hands on an analogue clock, make sure the hand that shows the hours is longer than the hand that shows the minutes. Hours are longer than minutes!

Reading times

Show these times on an analogue clock and a digital clock.

Bronze

1. half past three
2. eleven o'clock
3. half past nine
4. quarter past two
5. half past twelve
6. quarter to six
7. twelve o'clock
8. quarter past ten
9. quarter to four
10. half past five

Silver

1. twelve o'clock
2. quarter to six
3. twenty past ten
4. five past eight
5. quarter to two
6. twenty-five past four
7. half past six
8. ten past eleven
9. quarter to ten
10. twenty past two

Gold

1. quarter past eight
2. half past six
3. twenty to four
4. ten past eleven
5. quarter to twelve
6. five past one
7. twenty-five to seven
8. five to nine
9. ten to two
10. twenty-five past three

Training Tips

If the time is 'past' make sure the hour hand has gone past the hour.

If the time is 'to' make sure the hour hand is coming to the next hour.

Time problems

Being a referee means solving lots of time problems.

> *Example*
> The swimming races start at 3:45pm and last for
> an hour and a half.
> What time will they finish?
>
> One hour later would be 4:45pm.
> Another half an hour later makes it 5:15pm or
> quarter past five.

See if you can help the referees solve these problems.

Bronze

1. A hockey match started at ten o'clock and lasted for half an hour. What time did it finish?

2. A tennis game started at 2:30 and finished at 2:45. How long did it last?

3. The French swimming team practised from 11:45 until 12:15. How many minutes were they swimming for?

4. The long jump competition takes 30 minutes. If it finished at four o'clock, what time did it start?

5. The rugby match starts at half past ten. If it lasts for two and a half hours, what time will it end?

6. The high jump competition started at 5:15 and finished at quarter to six. How long did it last?

7. The rowing competition takes 45 minutes. It starts at 9:00. What time will it finish?

8. The gymnastics competition started at eight o'clock. There were three teams that each took an hour. What time did they finish?

Training Tips

Practise counting in fives. It will help you tell the time!

Remember there are 60 minutes in an hour.

Time problems

Silver

1. A hockey match started at half past ten and lasted for forty minutes. What time did it finish?

2. A tennis game started at 2:10pm and finished at 2:45pm. How long did it last?

3. The French swimming team practised from 11:40 until 1:00. How long were they swimming for?

4. A netball match started at 3:15pm and finished at five to four. How long did it last?

5. The long jump competition takes 50 minutes. If it finished at four o'clock, what time did it start?

6. The rugby match starts at half past ten. If it lasts for 80 minutes, what time will it end?

7. The rowing competition takes 1 hour and 25 minutes. It starts at nine o'clock. What time will it finish?

8. The gymnastics competition started at eight o'clock. There were three teams that each took an hour and a half. What time did they finish?

Gold

1. A hockey match started at quarter past ten and lasted for forty minutes. What time did it finish?

2. A tennis game started at 2:15pm and finished at 2:54pm. How long did it last?

3. The French swimming team practised from 11:05am until 1:25pm. How long were they swimming for?

4. A netball match started at 3:18pm and finished at five to four. How long did it last?

5. The long jump competition takes 1 hour and 50 minutes. If it finished at four o'clock, what time did it start?

6. The rugby match starts at quarter past ten. If it lasts for 80 minutes, what time will it end?

7. The rowing competition takes 2 hours and 25 minutes. It starts at half past nine. What time will it finish?

8. The gymnastics competition started at eight o'clock. There were three teams that each took an hour and a half. There were two breaks of 15 minutes each. What time did it finish?

2-D shapes

2-D shapes are flat shapes that can easily be drawn on paper.
They can be described by looking at the sides and the corners.
What shape has one curved side and no corners? ... A circle!

Write some clues to describe these shapes.
Make sure you are very clear in your description.
Try out your clues on a friend to see if you are good at describing.

 Bronze

1. triangle
2. circle
3. rectangle
4. square
5. pentagon
6. hexagon

 Silver

1. pentagon
2. semicircle
3. hexagon
4. oval
5. octagon
6. diamond

 Gold

1. quadrilateral
2. octagon
3. semicircle
4. star
5. oval
6. pentagon

Now draw some shapes.
You will need some dotted paper to help you
and a ruler to keep the lines straight.

Draw 5 different shapes with 4 straight sides. Can you name any of them?

Draw 5 different pentagons. Make sure all the sides are straight!

Draw 5 different quadrilaterals with at least one right angle.

 **Training Tips**

 An octopus has 8 legs and an octagon has 8 sides.

 Hexagon has an X in it and so does six. A hexagon is the shape with six sides.

3-D shapes

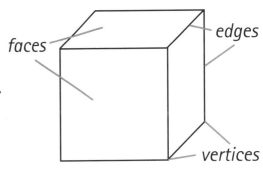

3-D shapes are fat shapes that are not so easy to draw. To describe them we need to think about the faces, the edges and the vertices (corners).

A cube has 6 square faces. It has 8 vertices and 12 edges.

faces   *edges*   *vertices*

Write some clues to describe these shapes. Remember to describe what the faces are like and how many edges and vertices they have.

 Bronze

1. cube
2. sphere
3. cylinder
4. cuboid
5. cone
6. pyramid

 Silver

1. cube
2. pyramid
3. hemisphere
4. sphere
5. prism
6. cylinder

 Gold

1. square-based pyramid
2. hemisphere
3. hexagonal prism
4. triangular-based pyramid
5. cube
6. triangular prism

Here are some activities for you to try.

Have a look around your classroom and see how many cuboids you can find. Write a list or draw a picture of them all.

Have a look around your classroom and see how many cylinders you can find. Write a list or draw a picture of them all.

Use 4 cubes and investigate all the different 3-D shapes you can make. Try drawing them.

 **Training Tips**

 To help remember the names, think about objects that are the same shape, such as an ice cream cone and the pyramids in Egypt.

Lines of symmetry

A line of symmetry is like looking in a mirror.
Both sides must be the same, like a reflection.

This triangle has only one line of symmetry
but a rectangle has two.

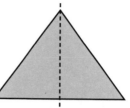 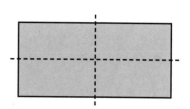

Copy the shapes below and draw in the lines of symmetry.
Some have only one line but some have two or even more!

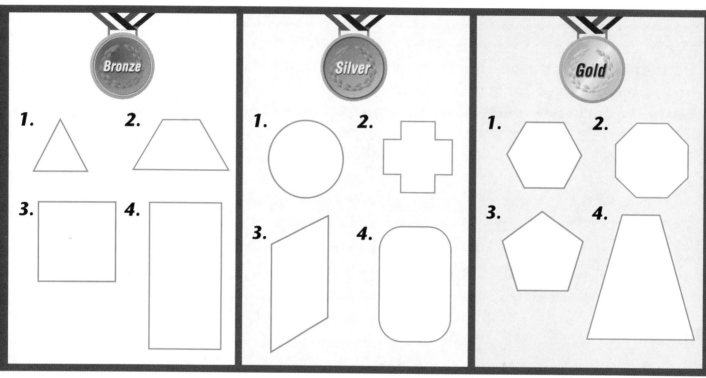

Bronze

1.   2.

3.   4.

Silver

1.   2.

3.   4.

Gold

1.   2.

3.   4.

The flags of most countries are symmetrical.
Copy and complete these flags making sure they are symmetrical.

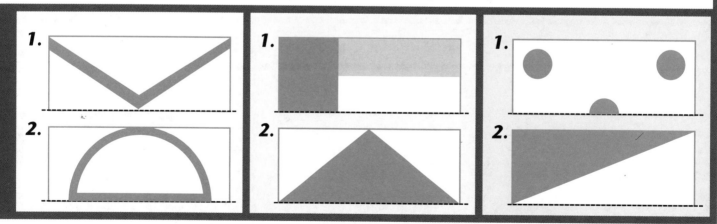

1.   1.   1.

2.   2.   2.

Training Tips

You could use a mirror to check before you draw.

Position and direction

Look at the grid below. We can describe where things are by using letters and numbers. Always give the letter first!

Ant Hill is at E8.

Coconut Grove is at L5.

We can use the compass points **north**, **south**, **east** and **west** to give directions from one place to another.

For example, to get from Ant Hill to Faraway Lagoon, we need to go 5 squares north and 1 square west.

Write directions to travel between the following places.

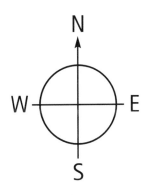

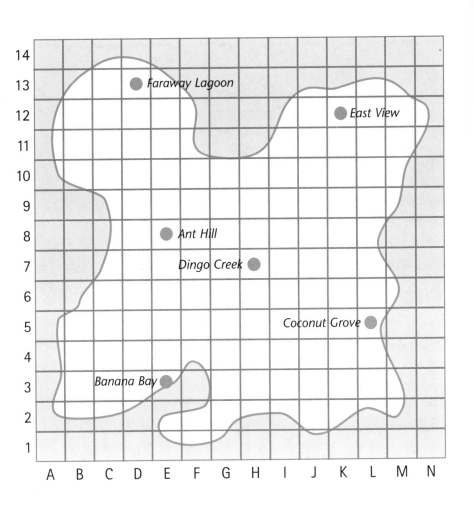

Bronze

Write directions to travel between **Ant Hill** and **East View.**

Silver

Write directions to travel from **Ant Hill** to **Dingo Creek** and then to **Banana Bay.**

Gold

Write directions to travel to each spot on the island starting at **Ant Hill** and ending at **Faraway Lagoon.**

Training Tips

 When finding a location, always go along first and then up.

Right angles

A quarter turn is also called a right angle.
Lots of 2-D shapes have right angles in them.

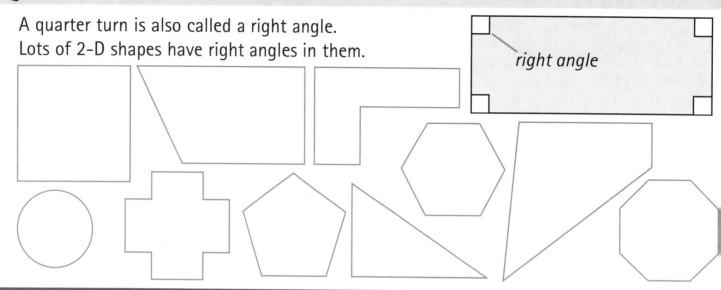

right angle

Look at the shapes above.
Sort them by looking at the right angles.
Draw them in the correct groups.

Bronze

1. Sort them into two groups:

A Shapes with some right angles and

B Shapes with no right angles

2. Colour all the right angles red.

Silver

1. Sort them into three groups:

A Shapes with all right angles

B Shapes with some right angles

C Shapes with no right angles

2. Colour all the right angles red.

Gold

1. Sort them into three groups. Some shapes may appear in more than one group:

A Shapes with angles less than a right angle

B Shapes with right angles

C Shapes with angles greater than a right angle

2. Colour all the right angles red.

What other shapes could you add to the groups you have made?

Training Tips

Use the corner of this book to check right angles.

A straight line is made up of two right angles!

Sorting information

The table below shows the scores from a rugby competition.

Japan 12	Norway 7	England 8	France 11	Spain 10
Switzerland 30	America 25	Turkey 13	Denmark 14	Russia 16
Iceland 20	Australia 15	Scotland 17	Ireland 20	Greece 16
Finland 25	China 19	Hong Kong 19	Egypt 18	Morocco 45
Germany 35	Holland 24	Canada 60	South Africa 45	Austria 27
Wales 42	Poland 65	Mexico 28	Sweden 70	Brazil 95

Bronze

Copy this Carroll diagram and sort the scores into the correct places.

Multiples of 5	Not multiples of 5
Spain 10	Norway 7

1. How many scores were not multiples of 5?

2. What score was the highest multiple of 5?

3. What was the lowest score that was not a multiple of 5?

4. How many multiples of 5 were also greater than 40?

5. How many scores less than 40 were not multiples of 5?

Silver

Copy this Carroll diagram and sort the scores into the correct places.

Odd numbers	Even numbers

1. How many odd numbers were greater than 40?

2. List the even numbers less than 40.

3. How many scores were odd numbers?

4. How many scores were less than 40?

5. What was the highest even number scored?

Gold

Copy this Venn diagram and sort the scores into the correct places.

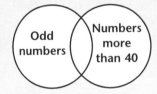

1. Which scores were odd numbers and also more than 40?

2. Which even numbers were more than 40?

3. Which odd numbers were less than 40?

4. How many teams scored more than 40?

5. List the numbers that did not fit in either circle. What did you notice about them?

Training Tips

 Cross off each number when you have sorted it.

Drawing bar charts

The table below shows the scores from a hockey competition.

Round 1		Round 2		Round 3	
Japan	7	Australia	12	Holland	40
Norway	12	Scotland	24	Canada	60
England	18	Ireland	15	Hong Kong	130
France	10	Switzerland	18	Austria	50
Spain	15	Greece	22	Wales	75
America	9	Finland	28	Poland	135
Turkey	8	China	19	South Africa	95
Denmark	14	Egypt	9	Mexico	80
Russia	15	Morocco	14	Sweden	115
Iceland	11	Germany	23	Brazil	145

Bronze

Draw a bar chart for Round 1. Draw the vertical axis up to 20 counting in ones. Write the names of the countries across the bottom axis.

1. Which country won Round 1?

2. Which country scored the least?

3. Which countries scored 15 points?

4. Which countries scored more than 10 points?

5. How many more points did Russia score than France?

6. How many fewer points did Iceland score than England?

7. Which countries scored an even number of points?

8. Which countries scored less than Norway?

9. How many more points did England score than America?

10. How many countries competed in Round 1?

Drawing bar charts

Silver

Draw a bar chart for Round 2. Draw the vertical axis up to 30 counting in twos. Write the names of the countries across the bottom axis.

1. Which country lost Round 2?

2. Which country scored the most?

3. Which countries scored between 10 and 20 points?

4. Which countries scored more than 17 points?

5. How many more points did Greece score than Morocco?

6. How many fewer points did Egypt score than Scotland?

7. Which countries scored an odd number of points?

8. Which countries scored less than Switzerland?

9. How many more points did Finland score than Australia?

10. How many fewer points did China score than Germany?

Gold

Draw a bar chart for Round 3. Draw the vertical axis up to 150 counting in tens. Write the names of the countries across the bottom axis.

1. Which country lost Round 3?

2. Which country scored the most points?

3. Which countries scored between 105 and 150 points?

4. Which countries scored less than 95 points?

5. How many more points did Hong Kong score than Holland?

6. How many fewer points did Mexico score than Sweden?

7. Which countries scored a multiple of 5?

8. Which countries scored more than Wales?

9. Which country scored twice as much as Holland?

10. Use the words most, least and difference to write three sentences about your bar chart.

Pictograms

A pictogram is a way of using pictures to show information.
All pictograms must have a key to show what each picture represents.

Example

This pictogram shows the number of gold medals that each country won.

Key ⚇ = 2 medals

Australia	⚇ ⚇ ⚇ ⚇
Scotland	⚇ ⚇ ⚇ ⚇ ⚇
Ireland	⚇ ⚇ ⚇

This pictogram show us that Australia won 8 gold medals,
Scotland won 10 gold medals and Ireland won 5 gold medals.

**Draw pictograms to show how many medals each country won.
Don't forget to give your pictogram a title.**

Bronze Key ⚇ = 1 medal		**Silver** Key ⚇ = 2 medals		**Gold** Key ⚇ = 4 medals	
Japan	6	Australia	18	Holland	16
Norway	11	Scotland	12	Canada	12
England	19	Ireland	16	Hong Kong	20
France	8	Switzerland	9	Austria	10
Spain	5	Greece	15	Wales	18
America	11	Finland	14	Poland	14
Turkey	12	China	7	South Africa	10
Denmark	14	Egypt	13	Mexico	6
Russia	10	Morocco	16	Sweden	9
Iceland	7	Germany	10	Brazil	17

Training Tips

If ⚇ = 2 medals then ⚇ = 1 medal.

Remember to put a key on your pictogram.